A Book Of

COMMERCIAL GEOGRAPHY

FY BBA (IB) (Semester - II)
Course Code - 203

(CBCS Pattern 2019)

As Per New Syllabus, Effective from June 2019

Prof. (Mrs.) P. N. PADEY
Former Head, Department of Geography,
Nowrosjee Wadia College,
Pune.

N4977

Commercial Geography ISBN 978-93-89825-30-5

First Edition : **January 2019**

© : **Author**

Published By:
NIRALI PRAKASHAN
Abhyudaya Pragati, 1312, Shivaji Nagar
Off J.M. Road, PUNE – 411005
Tel - (020) 25512336/37/39, Fax - (020) 25511379
Email : niralipune@pragationline.com

➢ **DISTRIBUTION CENTRES**

PUNE

Nirali Prakashan : 119, Budhwar Peth, Jogeshwari Mandir Lane, Pune 411002,
(For orders within Pune) Maharashtra, Tel : (020) 2445 2044, Mobile : 9657703145
Email : niralilocal@pragationline.com

Nirali Prakashan : S. No. 28/27, Dhayari, Near Asian College Pune 411041
(For orders outside Pune) Tel : (020) 24690204; Mobile : 9657703143
Email : bookorder@pragationline.com

MUMBAI

Nirali Prakashan : 385, S.V.P. Road, Rasdhara Co-op. Hsg. Society Ltd.,
Girgaum, Mumbai 400004, Maharashtra;
Mobile : 9320129587 Tel : (022) 2385 6339 / 2386 9976,
Fax : (022) 2386 9976
Email : niralimumbai@pragationline.com

➢ **DISTRIBUTION BRANCHES**

JALGAON

Nirali Prakashan : 34, V. V. Golani Market, Navi Peth, Jalgaon 425001,
Maharashtra, Tel : (0257) 222 0395, Mob : 94234 91860;
Email : niralijalgaon@pragationline.com

KOLHAPUR

Nirali Prakashan : New Mahadvar Road, Kedar Plaza, 1st Floor Opp. IDBI Bank,
Kolhapur 416 012, Maharashtra. Mob : 9850046155;
Email : niralikolhapur@pragationline.com

NAGPUR

Nirali Prakashan : Above Maratha Mandir, Shop No. 3, First Floor,
Rani Jhanshi Square, Sitabuldi, Nagpur 440012, Maharashtra
Tel : (0712) 254 7129;
Email : niralinagpur@pragationline.com

DELHI

Nirali Prakashan : 4593/15, Basement, Agarwal Lane, Ansari Road, Daryaganj
Near Times of India Building, New Delhi 110002
Mob : 08505972553, Email : niralidelhi@pragationline.com

BENGALURU

Nirali Prakashan : Maitri Ground Floor, Jaya Apartments, No. 99, 6th Cross,
6th Main, Malleswaram, Bengaluru 560003, Karnataka;
Mob : 9449043034
Email: niralibangalore@pragationline.com

Other Branches : Hyderabad, Chennai

niralipune@pragationline.com | www.pragationline.com
Also find us on   www.facebook.com/niralibooks

Preface ...

It gives me great pleasure to present the textbook of Commercial Geography to our FY BBA - IB students readers. This book has been designed as a standard text book on Commercial Geography.

This book covers the entire syllabus of FY BBA Semester II new course of Savitribai Phule Pune University, Pune effective from June 2019 onwards. This book has been written to fulfill the basic concepts. Some of the features of the book are observation, perception, analysis, critical thinking and understanding the relationship between natural resources and human society.

The book has been designed in four chapters. The basic idea behind this is to present the matter in a systematic way. First chapter deals with the Introduction to Commercial Geography, Nature and scope, Utility and aspects, various commercial sectors and Geographical indication. Second chapter deals with the Natural resources and its commercial usage in Indian context, meaning, nature and importance, forests, non-conventional energy resources.

Third chapter is on the role of Industries and Geographical significance in the Indian context. The chapter deals with role of Industries, Industrial location, Local localisation process, Rural and Handicraft Industries. Fourth and last chapter of this book is on Trade and Transportation importance salient features modes of transportations various routes and new trends.

Every effort has been made to provide accurate information on the subject. I am very grateful to our publisher **Shri. Dineshbhai Furia** and **Shri. Jigneshbhai Furia** who provided all assistance in the publication of this book. I wish to acknowledge my deep gratitude to staff members Mr. Arindam Haldar, Mr. Nitin Thorat, Mr. Ravindra Walodare and Mrs. Sarika Supekar who have helped in preparing this book. This book will prove useful to all the students and teachers of this subject.

Yours reviews and suggestions are always taken positively.

Mrs. P. N. PADEY
AUTHOR

PUNE
DECEMBER 2019

Syllabus ...

Commercial Geography : BBA (Sem-II) - Course Code 203

Commercial Geography : BBA (IB) : (Sem-II) -

Credits - 3

1. Introduction to Commercial Geography (Indian Context)

1. Definition, Nature and scope of Commercial Geography

2. Concept, Features, Role and Utility of Commercial Geography in Business and Economics

3. Major Aspects of Study in Commercial Geography

4. Commercial Sectors in the economy such as Primary, Secondary, Tertiary, Quaternary

5. Geographical Indications - Concept, Nature and Importance

2. Natural Resources and Commercial Usage (Indian Context)

1. Meaning, Nature and Importance

2. Types of Forests, Characteristics, Distribution and Significance

3. Non-Conventional Energy Resources - Solar, Wind and Tidal Energy

4. Commercial Usage and Role of Natural Resources in the development of Commerce

3. Role of Industries and Geographical Significance (Indian Context)

1. Role of Industries in the Economic Development and Factors affecting Industrial Location, Business Locations and it's Geographical Implications

2. Location - Need and Importance

3. Limitations to Local Localization Process and Sourcing of Location

4. Rural and Handicraft Industries - Economic and Commercial Importance

4. Trade and Transportations (Global Context)

1. Role and Importance of Trade

2. Importance of Transportation in Commercial Development - Salient Features, Merits and Limitations

3. Types of Modes of Transportation - Roadways, Railways, Airways, Seaways and Types of Trade Routes - Silk Route, CPCC etc.

4. New Trends in the Means and Modes of Transportation

Contents ...

Chapter 1...

Introduction to Commercial Geography (Indian Context)

Contents ...

1.1   Definition, Nature and Scope of Commercial Geography
    1.1.1   Definitions of Commercial Geography
    1.1.2   Nature of Commercial Geography
    1.1.3   Scope of Commercial Geography
1.2   Concept, Features, Role and Utility of Commercial Geography in Business and Economics
1.3   Major Aspects of Study in Commercial Geography
1.4   Commercial Sectors in the Economy such as Primary, Secondary, Tertiary, Quaternary
    1.4.1   Economic Activities of Man
1.5   Geographical Indications - Concept, Nature and Importance
- Points to Remember
- Questions for Discussion
- Questions from Previous Examinations

Learning Objectives ...

➤ To study the commercial activities showing different occupation in various environments.

➤ To study the diversity and physical conditions of the environment along with the social conditions.

➤ To study the spatial organisation of tertiary activities in the physical environment and the social consequences in a range of geographical scales.

INTRODUCTION

The word 'Geography' is derived from the Greek words "geo", meaning the earth and "graphe," meaning a description. Accordingly, Geography may be defined as the description of the earth. In earlier times, Geography was purely descriptive and used to describe places and the people. The nature of early maps was also different from today's maps. The early maps were interested in merely showing the locations of cities, towns, mountains and rivers.

"After 1850, the subject emerged in its real meaning. People were more interested in the distribution of crops, animals and trees over certain areas. Hence, they started asking why a particular area grows a particular crop ? Why conifers grow in temperate regions? Why laterites are concentrated only in the tropics ? This led to the origin of today's Causal Geography. Geographers started noting the causes behind and started noting their effects. Thus Modern Geography is not merely on of the surface of the earth along with natural and man-made features but it also includes the investigations in which Geographer also relates, organises and the phenomena of the earth.

Modern Geography is not only concerned with the earth, but also with man's relationship with the earth. It is a study of the natural environment and of man's relation to it. Man is the central point of geographical study.

Thus Geography studies many things : it deals with the origin and the interior of the earth: the distribution of land and water. the relief of the land-masses and the ocean floor: earth's atmosphere with its temperature, pressure, winds and moisture-, the different soils and vegetation: the different races and distribution of man: the resources of the earth and; their utilization by man and so on. Geography studies the physical as well as the human and economic aspects and their mutual relationship. Thus Geography may be said to study: the where ? and why ? of every natural and manmade resource on the earth.

Interaction of Geography With Other Subjects

Man's very existence on the surface of the earth depends on several natural resources; like air, water, soil, vegetation cover, animals, and minerals. He gets his livelihood from these resources by producing and processing them, by consuming them and by exchanging them. Naturally he is related to a number of aspects. His activities of mining depend on the, existence and extraction of minerals, on which again depends his major activity & manufacturing. Hence he is related to Geology. Man's life and his economic activities are. largely influenced by climatic conditions. These are responsible for his very existence, his living conditions over an area, the crops he grows, the clothes he wears, the food he eats and the commodities he trades and so on. Hence Geography is related to Meteorology. Man uses the large water bodies of oceans for his trade and transport and gets innumerable': valuable substances from it for his benefit, e.g. marine life, salt, minerals etc. Here Geography deals with Oceanography.

Though large areas of the surface of the earth are inhabited by man, the people living in different areas have different skin colour and they belong to different races like Negroid, Caucasoid, Aryans. Here Geography is related to Anthropology. Man extracts resources from the earth, processes them into more valuable items. Further, he exchanges these commodities with different commodities grown and processed in other areas. Thus, commodities flow from surplus areas to the deficit areas. Commodities are exchanged with, the help of various modes of transportation and with the help of financial assistance from various institutions like credit co-operative societies and banks. The commodities enter the wholesale and retail market and national or international market. Here Geography uses certain results of Economics. Man is a social animal and prefers to live in a group and here originates the social life of man, his traditions and. customs, the infinite variety of is settlements. that range from tiny hamlets to complicated megapolises. Here geography is related to Sociology.

Thus. Geography relies on results of sciences like Geology, Meteorology. Anthropology, Sociology and Economics because these are concerned with the environment of the central figure, man.

- Several authors have defined the term 'commerce' in their own way. Some of the major definitions are as follows :
- **According to Dr. Evlyin Thomas,** "Commerce' is a term that embraces all those functions involved in the making, buying, selling and transport of goods."
- **According to Stephenson,** "Commerce' constitutes the sum total of those processes, which are engaged in the removal of hindrances of persons, place and time, in the exchange of commodities."
- **According to Noel Branton**, "Commerce' comprises a group of specialised activities, which together form an essential part of the process of production. It links supplies and consumers by means of such as transport, banking, insurance, ware housing, advertising, publicity and en."
- These above definitions make it clear that, commerce is a wider term and includes in it the trade as well as various means which facilitate trade.

1.1 DEFINITION, NATURE AND SCOPE OF COMMERCIAL GEOGRAPHY

Modern Geography studies the relationship between man and his environment. It encompasses man's adaptation to the environment in which he lives and works. In 1891, the definition of Geography given by Ritter, Peschel and Ratzel is : "Geography as a whole is regarded as that department of knowledge which studies the varied features of the earth's surface as the environment of mankind". Thus, getting to know about one's environment and about each other is Geography.

1.1.1 Definitions of Commercial Geography

(i) Commercial Geography that deals with commodities according to their places of origin and their paths of transportation.

(ii) It is the study of commercial occupations of man.

(iii) Geography that deals with commodities according to their places of origin and their paths of transportation.

(iv) Commercial geography looks at trade and transitions in terms of what they involve, how they are generated and their outcomes.

(v) Commercial Geography investigates the spatial characteristics of trade and transactions in terms of their nature, causes and consequences. It leans on the analysis of transactions, from a simple commercial transaction involving an individual purchasing a product at a store to the complex network of transactions maintained between a multinational corporation and its suppliers. The scale and scope of commercial geography varies significantly.

(vi) Commercial geography is a form of geography concerned with the production and supply of raw materials including agricultural output and finished goods.

(vii) It is the study of the way man adjusts his economic activities to the physical environment.

1.1.2 Nature of Commercial Geography

- In a strict sense, Commercial Geography is the study of the commercial occupations of Man. Man engages himself in various economic activities like hunting, mining, agriculture, forestry, livestock rearing, manufacturing trade, transport, communication, tourism, etc. But all these economic activities are not commercial activities.

- Transportation, storage, export and imports, wholesale and retail trade are the commercial activities of man. The geography of these activities is known as Commercial Geography.

- According to Chisholm, "the main purpose of Commercial Geography is to create interest In the geographical facts related to commerce." Thus along with the commercial activities we have to include the geographical factors like major trade routes of the world, various modes of transportation, the location and situation of ports and their hinterlands, etc.

- If the exchange of goods is studied in Commercial Geography, then it is obvious that should know various areas that produce the different commodities. All areas on the surface of the earth do not produce all commodities.

- For example, the mineral resources are very unevenly distributed in the earth's crust. Thus some areas are rich in certain minerals while other areas may be poor in them. The tropical areas produce crop like wheat, sugarbeet, barley are grown in very few areas of the tropical lands only in winter.

- Thus tropical areas have surplus of tropical crops while temperate areas are deficit of these crops and vice-versa.

- Humid temperate areas of the world like the Netherlands, Denmark and Holland have large surplus of milk products. Temperate areas have coniferous forests which provide wood pulp to the world for making paper and synthetic fibres. Thus areas of excess production and the areas of scarcity both must be known.

- These two areas form the very foundation of trade and so the production of various commodities enters in Commercial Geography. Certain geographical factors are responsible for the production of these goods, They include physiography, climate, soil, manpower, machine etc.

- In order to get the knowledge of production of various commodities, one has to study these underlying factors also. Without a knowledge of these geographical facts, the study of only the distribution of various commodities will be superficial.

- Thus Commercial Geography is a study of geographical facts related to all kinds of economic activities such as production, consumption, distribution and exchange.

- As Commercial activities are closely related to other economic activities, such as production and consumption, Commercial Geography cannot be separated from its parent discipline of Economic Geography. According to B.S. Negi, the field of Commercial Geography is much wider than that of Economic Geography.

1.1.3 Scope of Commercial Geography

- Commercial Geography deals with the production, consumption and exchange of commodities. This very nature of Commercial Geography shows its importance in the field of commerce.
- World trade, whether it is international or national, depends mainly on demand and supply. The demand. for a commodity creates a market for it. Thus a businessman should first know about the demands of the people. These demands are many and varied. They come from deficit areas.
- These deficit areas are the results of the differences in natural and cultural environment, e.g. mountainous areas are unable to produce agricultural products on a large scale and hence the people living in such areas have to bring their necessary food-stuffs from the nearby plain areas. Usually the plains are not associated with beautiful natural landscape.
- Hence the people who live in the plains go to beautiful places situated in mountainous areas for recreation. The temperate lands of northern hemisphere create large market for wool. Economically developing countries have a constant demand for manufactured goods.
- Thus it is essential for a businessman to study the impact of natural and cultural environment which creates a demand for various commodities. Moreover, he should also come to know why these demands are created.
- Demand are various commodities is automatically followed by the supply. Certain areas are surplus areas for various commodities. e.g. temperate grasslands produce plenty of wheat, tropical highlands produce plenty of tea, plateaus are rich in a variety of minerals.
- The businessman should know these areas of surplus production and he should also know why they are able to produce these commodities on a large scale.
- The mass production comes to the market through various modes of transportation. It is essential to have a knowledge of the modes of transportation, their distribution in the world and the costs involved.
- People create a market. The market depends on the absolute number of people and their purchasing power. A knowledge of the density of population, the age structure of the people, and the various economic activities of man is essential to know the nature of world commerce.
- Many of the economic activities of man depend on natural resources. Usually these activities are resource oriented. Industries manufacturing paper pulp are located near the coniferous forests.
- Commercial fishing is carried out in the temperate parts of the oceans. Dairy creameries are located in areas of dairy farming. Hence a knowledge of the resources of the world is a must.
- Modern civilization has given rise to industrialisation. Numerous factors influence the location of industries. If the industrialist has a sound knowledge of -the resources, he will not set up a paper mill in a desert or in a grassland, nor he will set up an industry producing cars in a region which does not produce iron and steel.

- All the economic activities of man are responsible for the pollution of the environment. Beautiful landscapes are losing their vegetation cover; industrial wastes and sewage are finding their' outlets in water bodies; a large number of industries and automobiles are polluting the air by pouring out obnoxious gases into the atmosphere.
- At the present rate of air, water and land pollution the very existence of man will be in danger in the near future.
- Commercial Geography embraces all these fundamental and essential aspects and hence its study is essential to every man.

1.2 CONCEPT, FEATURES, ROLE AND UTILITY OF COMMERCIAL GEOGRAPHY IN BUSINESS AND ECONOMICS

Concepts :
- Commercial Geography is an important branch of Economic Geography. When we study Commercial Geography, we study all commercial activities in it. The activities which are related to trade are known as commercial activities. Commercial geography involves the production and utilization of commodities, the transport and communication and trade.
- According to Chisholm, it is an intellectual interest to the study of geographical facts relating to commerce.

Importance of Economic and Commercial Geography :
- Importance of economic and commercial geography can be derived from the following :
- **(a) Advantages for Students :** By studying economic and commercial geography students can become successful businessmen, industrialist, traders, landlords and bankers of the future.
- **(b) Advantages for Farmers :** With the help of study of commercial geography a farmer can know about the modern methods of cultivation, use of machine, better seeds and fertilizers. In this way a farmer can increase his productivity.
- **(c) Advantage for Industrialists of :** Commercial geography an industrialist can hire cheap labour, raw material for his industry. He can find new markets for his products. Thus by studying commercial geography an industrialist can be in position to do these things easily.
- **(d) Advantages for Traders :** The study of this subject can be helpful for traders in this sense that a trader comes to know from where he can achieve/get cheap raw material and also know those areas where such materials are use and sold.
- **(e) Helpful to Government Policy makers :** Economics geography represents the review of agricultural, industrial and economics development. Government can make effective planning in the light of developed countries to utilize the available agricultural, industrial and mineral resources.
- **(f) Reduction of Poverty and Unemployment :** It may help in pointing out those assist in removing resources that my the poverty and unemployment. So in light of this information about the sources and resources people can to migrate those areas where they will get employment.

(g) Import and Export Trade : Study of economic and commercial geography is most important for imports and export of commodities because it gives us information about the produces and products of different countries due to which one can be in position to evaluate the conditions for exports and imports of goods.

Significance of Commercial Geography :

* The environment influence the progress or development of commercial activities and the nature of these activities changes regionally.
* This type of study is useful for planning and development of commercial activities. As there is greater importance to such activities today, the study of commercial geography also has got increasing importance.
* The study has been benefited in the following ways :

(1) Encourages Production :

* The products are obtained from the economic activities. Various commodities are obtained from the primary and secondary occupations.
* The tertiary and quaternary activities are service help in the production and distribution process. The nature of production and services is different on regional level because they are abundant at some places and scarce at other. With the help of such information the decisions related to trade can be taken in commercial geography.
* The development of trade encourages the increase in the production and it helps in the regional economic development.

(2) Search for Markets :

* The regional information about productions helps in searching for markets. The origins of market are the regions of plenty, scarcity and specialised of productions.
* Their nature can be determined form the local level to international level. This information becomes useful in many globalization process.

(3) Motivation to Trade :

* There is no option to the exchange in the modern life style. The trade is standing as the base in the development of all economic activities. Therefore a competition in the development of trade exists.
* The production is very much beneficial to trade, The trade may be systematically developed with the help of such information.

(4) Development of Transport and Communication:

* The future of trade depends of the transport and communication system. Unless the transport system is cheap, safe and speedy, the trade can not develop.

(5) Development of Services :

* The trade establishes the relations among the regions. In this connection, the services are developed and employments are generated. The well educated and efficient (skilled) manpower gets employment opportunities. This begins the free movement of manpower. The service sector has been developing all over the world due to the modern life style of man.

1.3 MAJOR ASPECTS OF STUDY IN COMMERCIAL GEOGRAPHY

There are three approaches to the study of Commercial Geography :

(1) Regional Approach

- This approach describes and explains a region from the point of view of the economic activities of man. A region maybe classified as climatic, natural, geographical or political region. Political regions can change their boundaries. Only few years back East Pakistan was a part of Pakistan. Then it became separate from Pakistan and formed a new country called Bangaladesh.
- Thus political regions can change. But geographical regions are fixed and are not subject to change. If more than two political units are located in one geographical region, the two political units may not necessarily show the same degree of development, as the development of a region is the result of man's efforts.
- Take the example of Equatorial regions. The regions located in South America and Africa are in economically backward state. But the equatorial regions of South-East Asia have developed their agriculture economy on a large scale through commercial plantation agriculture.

(2) The Commodity Approach

- This approach is related to the production, distribution and utilization of a commodity, e.g. crops or minerals. These resources are described and explained not only at one particulars point of time, but with the whole sequence of their development.
- The farmers in the U.S.A. came to know that higher yields of cotton and better quality fibres can be obtained in semi-arid and, even and conditions with the use of irrigation.
- Hence they shifted cotton cultivation towards the western drier Prairie areas and brought land under its cultivation.
- Similarly along the same lines, the Russian Government brought large areas of central Asia under cotton cultivation, where soils are fertile, climatic conditions are semi-arid and litigation facilities are available.
- Today about 90% of the total Russian production of cotton comes from Central Asia. This approach is useful for growing a variety of resources in similar environmental conditions.

(3) Principle Approach

- In this approach, certain theories are established after a careful study of economic development of various countries or regions. These theories are based on man and his relationship with the environment e.g. the density of the network of roads and railways is more in plains than mountains, or the people living in the West European type of climate are more energetic, etc.
- Such theories are useful in finding out the relationship between the cause and effect. But it is not necessary that these theories are equally applicable to all countries of the world. All sorts of variations in the economic development are found and hence many a time these theories prove inadequate and inappropriate.

- All these approaches throw light on the degree of economic development of the region. Each approach has its limitations. But in respect of man and his environment, principle approach is more suitable while for the economic development of a region, regional approach is suitable. Man is at liberty to choose the approach according to his convenience.

1.4   COMMERCIAL SECTORS IN THE ECONOMY SUCH AS PRIMARY, SECONDARY, TERTIARY, QUATERNARY

1.4.1   Economic Activities of Man

Economic Activities of Man

- The economic activities of man involve the production, exchange and consumption of goods as well as the services needed to satisfy his basic, economic, social and intellectual needs.
- On the basis of the nature of work undertaken and the stage in the production process, we can classify economic activities into four basic types : (1) Primary activities (2) Secondary activities (3) Tertiary activities (4) Quaternary activities.

(1) Primary Activities :

- In primary sector of economy, activities are undertaken by **directly using natural resources** i.e. agriculture, mining, fishing, forestry, dairy etc. are some examples of this sector.
- **Forms the base for all other products**. Since most of the natural products we get are from agriculture, dairy, forestry, fishing, it is also called Agriculture and allied sector.
- People engaged in primary activities are called **red-collar workers** due to the outdoor nature of their work.
- Primary activities include all activities which extract natural resources from the earth. Hunting, fishing, lumbering, mining. agriculture, herding of livestock are all primary activities of man.
- These activities are fundamental and support other commercial activities. These activities depend on physical and manmade factors, e. g. lumbering depends on the existence of forests, the climate of the forested region, the physiography of these areas as well as on the availability of labour, adequate transportation facilities, distance from the market and several other factors.
- The activity of mining depends on the existence of minerals in the earth's crust, the nature of the mineral ore, the depth of the mineral-bearing strata, the relief and climate of the region as well as the technology of mining, transportation facilities, distance from market, etc.
- The percentage of people engaged in primary activities varies greatly in different countries of the world. More people are engaged in these activities in the developing countries like Afghanistan, Laos, Kampuchea and India.

- Agriculture is the major primary activity of man and nearly 50% of the working population of the world is engaged in agriculture. In the highly industrialised countries of the world, the percentage of the working population engaged in primary activities is less, e. g. Germany, France, the U. K. and the U. S. A.

(2) Secondary Activities :

- This sector includes the industries where finished products are derived from natural materials produced in the primary sector i.e. industrial production, cotton fabric, sugar cane production etc.
- Hence it is that part of the country's economy which manufactures goods, rather than producing raw materials. People engaged in secondary activities are called blue collar workers.

Examples of manufacturing sector :

1. Small workshops producing pots, artisan production.
2. Mills producing textiles,
3. Factories producing steel, chemicals, plastic, and so on.
4. Food production such as brewing plants, and food processing.
5. Oil refinery.

- Eight core industries are electricity, steel, refinery products, crude oil, coal, cement, natural gas and fertilizers.
- The products obtained from primary activities are collected and are transformed into more useful forms through a process known as manufacturing. For instance, cotton cultivation is a primary activity while the manufacturing" of cotton cloth is a secondary activity. Manufacturing is a complex activity.
- The finished product from one firm often forms the raw materials for another firm, e.g. the finished product of an iron and steel industry is steel, which in turn, is the raw material for the automobile industry.
- The economic activity of manufacturing depends on several factors, like the availability of raw material, labour force, power resources, transportation facilities, government policy, capital, physiography and climate of the region and several others.
- That is why manufacturing has not developed at the same rate in all the countries of the world. Due to favourable factors, this economic activity is developed largely in the north-eastern parts of the U. S. A., in the Western and central core of Europe, in the western third of the Russian Federation and in southern Japan.
- The percentage of working people engaged in manufacturing is more in these areas while it is much less in many developing countries of tropical Africa, South America and South-East Asia.

(3) Tertiary Activities :

- This sector's activities is complementary to the development of the primary and secondary sectors. Economic activities in tertiary sector do not produce goods but they are an aid or a support for the production.
- Goods transportation banking, insurance, finance etc. come under the sector.

- Tertiary sector jobs are called white collar jobs.
- Pink-collar worker is one who is employed in a job that is traditionally considered to be women's work.
- A pink collar worker is usually a woman. Men rarely work in pink collar jobs. Some examples of pink collar occupations are baby sitter, florist, day care worker, nurses etc.
- Lately, the pink collar worker is educated or trained. Pink collar workers are educated through training seminars or classes and they have to continue to strive for advancement in their careers.
- Today, women have more opportunities in traditionally male white-collar jobs and men work in traditionally female pink-collar jobs.
- Sunrise industry is a term used for a sector that is just in its infancy but shows promise of a rapid boom.
- The industry is typically characterized by high growth rates, high degree of innovation and generally has plenty of public awareness about the sector and investors get attracted to its long-term growth prospects.
- Existing Indian sectors that can be termed as Sunrise sectors and likely to hold us in good stead in the future in terms of employment generation and business growth are:

Information Technology :
1. Telecom Sector
2. Healthcare
3. Infrastructure Sector
4. Retail Sector
5. Food Processing Industries
6. Fisheries

- The tertiary activities of man include trade, transport, communication, and services. These activities are also known as non-productive occupations, as they are not concerned with any physical production of goods, like that of mining, agriculture or manufacturing.
- A large number of people are engaged in retail and wholesale trade, in transport, in communication services like posts and telephone offices and specialised services like lawyers, doctors and teachers.
- Thus, tertiary services embrace a variety of occupations, i. e. retail merchants, clerks, wholesale distributors, government employees, teachers, lawyers, bankers, insurance agents, electricians, telephone operators, carpenters, household servants, photographers, actors, musicians and several others.
- The number of people engaged in tertiary activities varies greatly, as it is directly dependent on the economic development of a country. In highly developed countries like the U. S. A. and in many of the West European countries, the proportion of people engaged in tertiary activities is very large.
- The number of people engaged in tertiary activities is always more in large cities and towns. Thus like industries, these activities also agglomerate in urban areas.

(4) Quarternary Activities :

- Quarternary activities are specialized tertiary activities in the **'Knowledge Sector'** which demands a separate classification.
- The quaternary sector is the intellectual aspect of the economy. It is the process which enables entrepreneurs to innovate and improve the quality of services offered in the economy i.e. Personnel working in office buildings, elementary schools and university classrooms, hospitals and doctors' offices, theatres, accounting and brokerage firms all belong to this category of services.
- Like other tertiary functions, quaternary activities can also be outsourced.

(5) Quinary Activities :

- In this sector the top-level decisions are made. This includes the government which passes legislation. It also consists of the top decision-makers in industry, commerce and also the education sector.
- These are services that focus on the creation, re-arrangement and interpretation of new and existing ideas; data interpretation and the use and evaluation of new technologies.
- Profession under this category called 'gold collar' professions, and they represent subdivision of the tertiary sector representing special and highly paid skills of senior business executives, government officials, research scientists, financial and legal consultants, etc.
- Quarteranary activities represent a special type of service work. They focus on professional and administrative services including financial and health services work, Information processing, teaching, government services as well as entertainment activities.
- These activities require specialised technical and leadership skills. All of them occur in office building environments or in specialised environments likes schools, hotels, hospitals or theatres. The people engaged in these activities are called as "white collar work force."

1.5 GEOGRAPHICAL INDICATIONS - CONCEPT, NATURE AND IMPORTANCE

Geographical Indication (Meaning) :

- A geographical indication (GI) is a sign used on products that have a specific geographical origin and possess qualities or a reputation that are due to that origin.
- Additionally the qualities, characteristics or reputation of the product should be essentially belong to the place of origin.

Geographical Indication Right :

- A geographical indication right enables those who have the right to use the indication to prevent its use by a third party whose product does not conform to the applicable standards.
- For example, the Darjeeling producers of Darjeeling tea can exclude use of the term "Darjeeling" for tea not grown in their tea gardens or not produced according to the standards set out in the code of practice for the geographical indication.

- However, a protected geographical indication does not allow the holder to prevent someone from making a product using the same methods as those set out in the standards for that indication.
- Geographical indications are used for agricultural products, foodstuffs, wine and spirit drinks, handicrafts, and industrial products.

Following are the ways to protect a geographical indication :

(i) So-called sui generis systems (i.e. special regimes of protection);
(ii) Using collective or certification marks; and
(ii) Methods focusing on business practices, including administrative product approval schemes.

- Generally, speaking geographical indications are protected in countries and regional systems through many approaches and often using a combination of two or more of the approaches outlined above.
- "Geographical indications are the signs given to natural products, metals, agricultural products, handicrafts and industrial products which distinguish themselves from other products by their distinctive qualities and which are identified with the area or region in which they are located.
- Geographical indications provide protection for products that have a certain fame in terms of certain local characteristics such as production and resource.
- Qualities such as naturalness, tradition, sustainable quality, regional development and the guarantee of being competitive on the world market are included in the added value that geographical indications offer.
- The geographical indication application may be carried out by real or legal persons and consumer associations producing the product subject to geographical indication and by public entities which are related to the subject and geographical area.
- A geographical indication is used to identify a product identified with a locality, area, region or country.
- These signs prevent third parties from misleading society and unfair competition. They prevent the creation of a sense that a product is produced locally, regionally or in an area-specific manner when it is not produced in that region or area.

Geographical Indication :

(i) It is an indication
(ii) It originates from a definite geographical territory.
(iii) It is used to identify agricultural, natural or manufactured goods
(iv) The manufactured goods should be produced or processed or prepared in that territory.
(v) It should have a special quality or reputation or other characteristics

Examples of Indian Geographical Indications :

- Basmati Rice
- Darjeeling Tea
- Kanchipuram silk saree
- Nagpur orange
- Kolhapuri chappal

- Bikaneri bhujia
- Agra petha

Registration of Geographical Indications :

- In December 1999, the Parliament had passed the Geographical Indications of Goods (Registration and Protection) Act,1999.
- This Act seeks to provide for the registration and better protection of geographical indications relating to goods in India.
- The Act would be administered by the Controller General of Patents, Designs and Trade Marks- who is the Registrar of Geographical Indications. The Act has come into force with effect from 15th September 2003.

Benefit of Registration of Geographical Indications :

(i)   It confers legal protection to Geographical Indications in India
(ii) Prevents unauthorised use of a Registered Geographical Indication by others
(iii) Provides legal protection to Indian Geographical Indications which in turn boost exports.
(iv) Promotes economic prosperity of producers of goods produced in a geographical territory.

Indications are not registrable :

- For registrability, the indications must fall within the Purview of 2(1)e of GI Act, 1999. It has to also satisfy the provisions of Section 9, which prohibits registration of a Geographical Indication.
- The use of which would be likely to deceive or cause confusion; or
- The use of which would be contrary to any law for the time being in force; or
- Which comprises or contains scandalous or obscene matter; or
- Which comprises or contains any matter likely to hurt the time being in force; religious susceptibilities of any class or section of the citizens of India; or
- Which would otherwise be dismantled to protection in a court; or
- Which are determined to be generic names or indications of goods and are, therefore, not or ceased to be protected in their country of origin or which have fallen into disuse in that country; or
- Which although literally true as to the territory region or locality in which the goods originate, but falsely represent to the persons that the goods originate in another territory, region or locality as the case may be.
- If a registered geographical indication is not renewed it is liable to be removed from the registar.

Geographical Indication Infringement :

- When an unauthorised user uses a geographical indication that indicates or suggests that such goods originate in a geographical area other than the true place of origin of such goods in a manner which mislead the public as to the geographical origin of such goods. When the use of geographical indication result in an unfair competition including passing off in respect of registered geographical indication. When the use of another geographical indication results in false representation to the public that goods originate in a territory in respect of which a registered geographical indication relates.

- The registered proprietor or authorised users of a registered geographical indication can initiate an infringement action.

Registration Process :

1. **Online filing of application :**
- To file an online application,
- The applicants need to first check whether the indication comes within the ambit of the definition of a GI under Section 2(1)(e).
- The applicant must have an address for service in India. Generally, application can be filed by (1) a legal practitioner (2) a registered agent.

2. **Track the status of application:**
- The status of all GI applications in India can be accessed at :
3. Preliminary scrutiny and examination will be done by Examiners.
4. Every application, within three moths of acceptance shall be published in the Geographical Indications Journal. Any person can file a notice of opposition within three months (extendable by another month on request which has to be filed before three months) opposing the GI application published in the Journal.
5. Where an application for a GI has been accepted, the registrar shall register the geographical indication. If registered the date of filing of the application shall be deemed to be the date of registration.

Geographical indication

- Geographical Indications protection is granted through the TRIPS Agreement.
- The consumer-benefit purpose of the protection rights granted to the beneficiaries has similarities and differences to the trade mark rights:

(a) While comparable goods are registered with GIs, similar goods and services are registered with trade marks.

(b) While GIs confer a geographical origin of a good, trade marks confer a commercial origin of an enterprise.

(c) While a GI is a name characterised by tradition from a delineated area, a trade mark is a sign as a badge of origin for goods and services.

(d) While a GI is a collective entitlement of public-private partnership, a trade mark refers entirely to private rights. With GIs, the beneficiaries are always a community from which usually, regardless of who is indicated in the register as applicant, they have the right to use. Trade marks distinguish goods and services between different undertakings, thus it is more individual (except collective trade marks which are still more private).

(e) While with GIs its particular quality is essential because of the geographical area, although the human factor may also play a part (collectively), with trade marks, even if there is any link to quality, it is essentially because of the producer and provider (individually).

(f) While GIs are an already existing expression and is used by existing producers or traders, a trade mark is usually a new word or logo chosen arbitrarily.

(g) While GIs are usually only for products, trademarks are for products and services.

(h) While GIs cannot become numerous by definition, with trade marks there is no limit to the number that can be possibly be registered or used.

(i) While GIs may not normally qualify as trade marks because they are either descriptive or misleading and distinguish products from one region from those of another, trade marks normally do not constitute a geographical name as there is no essential link with the geographical origin of goods.

(j) While GIs protect names designating the origin of goods, trade marks – collective and certification marks where a GI sui generis system exists – protect signs or indications.

(k) While with GIs there is no conceptual uniform approach of protection (public law and private law / sui generis law and common law), the trade mark concepts of protection are practically the same in all countries of the world (i.e., basic global understanding of the Madrid System). In other words, with GIs there is no international global consensus for protection other than TRIPS.

(l) While with GIs the administrative action is through public law, the enforcement by the interested parties of trade marks is through private law.

(m) While GIs are very attractive for developing countries rich in traditional knowledge, the new world, e.g., Australia, with a different industry development model they are more prone to benefit from trade marks. In the new world, GI names from abroad arrive through immigrants and colonisation, leading to generic names deriving from the GIs from the old world.

(n) While GIs lack a truly global registration system, trade marks global registration system is through the Madrid Agreement and Protocol.

- Rural development impacts from geographical indications, referring to environmental protection, economic development and social well-being, can be :

(i) The strengthening of sustainable local food production and supply (except for non-agricultural GIs such as handicrafts);

(ii) A structuring of the supply chain around a common product reputation linked to origin;

(iii) Greater bargaining power to raw material producers for better distribution so as for them to receive a higher retail price benefit percentage;

(iv) Capacity of producers to invest economic gains into higher quality to access niche markets, improving circular economy means throughout the value chain, protection against infringements such as free-riding from illegitimate producers, etc.;

(v) Economic resilience in terms of increased and stabilised prices for the GI product to avoid the commodity trap through de-commodisation, or to prevent/minimise external shocks affecting the premium price percentage gains (usually varying from 20-25%);

(vi) Added value throughout the supply chain;

(vii) Spill-over effects such as new business and even other GI registrations;

(viii) Preservation of the natural resources on which the product is based and therefore protect the environment;

(ix) Preservation of traditions and traditional knowledge;

(x) Identity based prestige;

(xi) Linkages to tourism.

- None of these impacts are guaranteed and they depend on numerous factors.
- Similar to trade marks, geographical indications are regulated locally by each country because conditions of registration such as differences in the generic use of terms vary from country to country.
- International trade made it important to try to harmonize the different approaches and standards that governments used to register GIs. The first attempts to do so were found in the Paris Convention on trademarks (1883, still in force, 176 members), followed by a much more elaborate provision in the 1958 Lisbon Agreement on the Protection of Appellations of Origin and their Registration. (28 countries are parties to the Lisbon agreement).
1. Article 22 of the TRIPS Agreement says that all governments must provide legal opportunities in their own laws for the owner of a GI registered in that country to prevent the use of marks that mislead the public as to the geographical origin of the good.
2. Article 23 of the TRIPS Agreement says that all governments must provide the owners of GI the right, under their laws, to prevent the use of a geographical indication identifying wines not originating in the place indicated by the geographical indication.
3. Article 24 of TRIPS provides a number of exceptions to the protection of geographical indications that are particularly relevant for geographical indications for wines and spirits (Article 23).
- In the Doha Development Round of WTO negotiations, launched in December 2001, WTO member governments are negotiating on the creation of a 'multilateral register' of geographical indications.
- Some governments participating in the negotiations (especially the European Communities) wish to go further and negotiate the inclusion of GIs on products other than wines and spirits under Article 23 of TRIPS.
- In India are products which have two geographical indications, one for the name and another for the logo.

Points to Remember

- The words 'Geography is derived from the Greek works "geo" meaning the earth and 'Graph".
- "Commerce" is a term that embraces all those functions involved in the making, buying, selling and transport of goods.
- Commercial Geography deals with the production, consumption and exchange of commodities.

- Three approaches to commercial Geography :
  (i)   Regional Approach
  (ii) The commodity Approach
  (iii) Principle Approach
- Primary activities includes all activities which extract natural resources from the earth i.e. Hunting. fishing, lumbering etc.
- When products are obtained from Primary activities are transformed into more useful forms.
- Significance of Commercial Geography : Study helps in
  (i)   Encourages production
  (ii) Search for Markets
  (iii) Motivation to trade
  (iv) Development of Transport and communication.
  (v)   Development of Services
- A Geographical indication (41) is a sign used on products that have a specific geographical origin and posses qualities or a reputation that are due to that origin.

Questions for Discussion

Q. (I) Answer the following questions :
1. Define Commercial Geography. State the nature of Commercial Geography.
2. State the scope of commercial geography.
3. What are the different approaches to the study of Commercial Geography ?
4. What do you understand by Primary sector activities ?
5. What do you understand by Secondary sector activities ?
6. What do you understand by the Tertiary sector in Indian economy ?
7. What do you understand by the Quaternary activities ?
8. Write a note on the importance of Economic and Commercial Geography.
9. What is the concept of Geographical Indication ?

Q. (II) Short Notes :
1. Commercial Geography
2. Importance of Commercial Geography
3. Primary Sector
4. Secondary Sector
5. Tertiary Sector
6. Quaternary Sector
7. Quinary Sector
8. Geographical Indication

Chapter **2**...

Natural Resources and Commercial Usage (Indian Context)

Contents ...

Learning Objectives ...

- ➢ To study and understand the importance of natural resources.
- ➢ To study and understand the role of natural resources and its role on development of the economy.
- ➢ To understand the importance of utilization of natural resources.
- ➢ To understand it's commercial use towards the growth of the economy sector.

INTRODUCTION

Natural resources exist on Earth without the indulgence of human Earth. It includes sunlight, atmosphere, water, land with all vegetation, crops and animal life that naturally exist on earth.

Natural resources are categorised in different ways. They are materials and components which can be found in the environment. Every man-made product is composed of natural resources. A natural resource may exist as a separate entity i.e. fresh water, air, and any living organism or it may exist in a different form such as rare earth metal, material, ores, petroleum, and energy.

Classification of Natural Resources

The various methods of categorizing natural resources include source of origin, stage of development, and by their renewability.

(i) Source of Origin :

- On this basis natural resources can be categorised into the following types:

    (a) Biotic : These resources are available in the biosphere (living and organic material), such as forests and animals, and the materials that can be obtained from them. Fossil fuels such as coal and petroleum are included in these sources.

    (b) Abiotic : These resources come from non-living, non-organic material. i.e. land, fresh water, air, rare earth metals and heavy metals including ores, gold, iron, silver, copper, etc.

(ii) Stage of Development :

Natural resources may be referred to in the following ways on the basis of the criteria :

    (a) Potential resources : Resources that may be used in the future—for example, petroleum.

    (b) Actual resources : Resources that have been surveyed, quantified and qualified and, are currently used i.e. wood processing, depends on technology and cost

    (c) Reserve resources : That part of an actual resource which can be developed profitably in the future

    (d) Stock resources : These resources that have been surveyed, but cannot be used due to lack of technology—for example, hydrogen

(iii) Renewability :

- On the basis of renewability following are the resources :

    (a) Renewable resources :

These resources are renewable and can be replenished naturally. These include sunlight, air, wind, water, etc. are continuously available and their quantities are not noticeably affected by human consumption. However these resources are susceptible to depletion by over-use. Resources are renewable so long as the rate of replenishment/recovery exceeds that of the rate of consumption. They replenish easily as compared to non-renewable resources.

    (b) Non-renewable resources : These resources form very slowly or do not form in the environment such as minerals. Resources are non-renewable when their rate of consumption is more than the rate of replenishment/recovery; i.e. fossil fuels, rate of formation is extremely slow (potentially millions of years), are considered non-renewable. Some resources naturally deplete such as radio-active elements like uranium, and decay into heavy metals. Coal and petroleum cannot be recycled. Once they are completely used they take millions of years to replenish.

2.1   MEANING, NATURE AND IMPORTANCE

2.1.1 Meaning of Resources

Prof. Zimmermann has defined resources as follows :

"Resource does not refer to a thing or a substance but to a function which a thing or a substance may perform, or to an operation in which it may take part".

- This definition gives a clear idea of resources :
  (1) Firstly, resources are related to man.
  (2) They are functional.

- Unless and until a thing or a substance does not satisfy human wants, it does not become a resource. Physical environment or nature is a 'neutral stuff, and it is human culture that determines which elements in nature are considered to be 'resources'. Take the example of minerals. For the past several geological ages they have been existing in the crust of the earth. Pre- historic man did not know about the vast deposits of these minerals and he did not know how to use them.

- At that time minerals were neutral stuffs. Afterwards man gained the knowledge of these minerals. He learnt their uses and then only minerals become 'resources'. Thus unless and until a thing or a substance does not satisfy human wants, it does not become a 'resource'. Substances are not resources. They become resources through man's use of them. The concept of resources in purely functional, inseparable from human wants and human capabilities.

2.1.2 Nature of Natural Resources

- Resources, are not static but are dynamic. Resources increase in number due to unlimited needs of man. Take into consideration the field of transportation. In ancient time, man used different animals for transportation. Then the draught animals were replaced by automobiles which used oil, coal and electricity as power resources. e.g cars, railways and aeroplanes. Now, in future, the place of these power resources will be taken by solar energy or some other inexhaustible power resources.

- With increased knowledge, expanding science, technical advancement, the resources either gain or lose their importance. In 1900, coal was a major power resource and its contribution to world fuel requirement was 98 per cent while oil and gas contributed only 1% of the fuel requirement. But, afterwards inspite of increasing production, coal has shown a steady decline in importance. Today coal supplies are about only 20% of the world's energy requirements while oil and natural gas are in great demand and supply about 71% of energy requirements.

- Many natural resources are exhaustible but some of them are renewable. If they are used on a large scale, without renewing them, these resources dwindle, e.g. forests. According to the report by Myers, Africa has lost 52% of its equatorial forest, Latin America 37% and South - East Asia 38%. On the other hand, Finland has about 75% of the land under forest. Forest management is science. Lumbering is practiced on a large scale, but at the same time more land is brought under forest. The farmers in Finland are encouraged to give up farming in which profits are less and turn their land over to forestation in order to increase the forest area.

- Some resources are inexhaustible and unchangeable. Ocean water, wind power, solar and climate belong to this type.
- Some exhaustible resources are re-usable. Most of the metals like iron, tin, copper, and silver are of this type. Iron ore is used on a large scale for manufacturing steel. Old - machinery and scrap is used again for manufacturing more steel.
- Exhaustible resources include coal, petroleum, natural gas and most non-metallics. Once these resources are used up, they cannot be replaced in nature.
- Distribution of resources is highly uneven. For example, the distribution of minerals. Some areas are rich in these resources, e.g. Republic of South Africa, the Chhota Nagpur plateau in India; while some areas are deficient in minerals, e.g. Sri Lanka and Bangladesh. The intensity of solar energy is more in the tropical lands of the world and it gradually diminishes towards both poles. Many areas are deficient in forest resources, e.g. the polar areas, deserts, upper slopes of mountains, etc. To some extent the uneven distribution of resources is responsible for the uneven economic development in the world.

Classification of Resources :

On the *basis of their aims and purposes*, resources are classified in different ways. Basically, resources can be divided into two types :

(i) Natural resources

- The resources that are made available by nature come in this category. They include land, soil, minerals like coal, iron-ore, oil, gold, rocks of economic value like granite, limestone, forests, natural grasslands, animal life, marine life and water.

(ii) Human resources

- These resources are considered in two ways - by studying the quantity of population and secondly by studying their quality.
- Quantitative resources include total number of people, density of population, age group and age-structure and actual percentage of working population.
- Qualitative resources include man's intelligence, imagination, skill, personality, education and several other qualities which are responsible for the economic development of a region.

Classification of Natural Resources :

- **Renner** has classified natural resources into two groups :

(i) Inexhaustible resources

- These resources are also known as flow resources. When the supply of natural resources is continuous and permanent, the natural resources are inexhaustible resources e.g. water, air, solar energy, etc.

(ii) Exhaustible resources

- These resources have limited fixed reserves. Once they are used, man is unable to replace them. They are also known as fund resources. They include resources like minerals. Both these natural resources are divided into six distinct categories :

(1) Inexhaustible and unchangeable resources : These resources get renewed on their own after some time. They include ocean water, wind power, solar power. Take the example of ocean water. Evaporation takes place from oceans and this water vapour is carried by the winds to the land in the form of clouds. The clouds give rainfall. This water again flows towards the ocean in the form of ground-water and rivers. Thus the total amount of water in the oceans remains unchanged.

(2) Inexhaustible but misusable resources : They include water, surface water bodies, area, space, etc. Industrial wastes normally find their outlet into rivers, lakes and seas. The residues of the manufacturing processes are dumped into these water-bodies. The water gets polluted. Thus these resources are misused.

(3) Maintainable and Renewable resources : These resources include human numbers, land fertility, timber, ground water, etc. When the trees are cut, new tress can be planted again. The fertility of the soil can be maintained with the help of fertilizers. Human numbers can be checked by controlling the birth rate.

(4) Maintainable but Non-renewable resources : These resources include wild animals, trees, many forms of fish, human talent and genius.

(5) Exhaustible but Re-usable resources : Gems, some non-metallic minerals, and metals like, tin, gold and silver come under this category. For example, the machinery made from steel becomes old and useless after some time. This machinery is used as scrap for making new steel. Thus this resource can be used again.

6. Exhaustible, one use resource : Coal, petroleum, natural gas and certain metals belong to this category. Once they are used, they are gone forever. Once coal or oil is burnt, man is unable to replace them.

Classification of Resources *(based on their distribution)*

- On the basis of distribution, resources may be localized or they may be ubiquitous. Localized resources are found at specific places. They have great influence on the development of economic activities of man. These resources are coal, iron-ore, bauxite and several others. Iron and steel industries of India are concentrated mainly in the three states place - Bihar, Orissa and West Bengal, because these three states are very rich in basic resources like iron and coal. But certain resources are ubiquitous, i.e. they are found everywhere e.g. oxygen in air.

The *nature of ownership of resources* classifies them into three categories :

(1) Individual resources : Individual or personal resources are those that are exploited or utilized for individual benefit only. Material possessions like cash, land, etc. and human skill, knowledge and good health belong to this category.

(2) National resources : These resources are owned collectively by a nation., e.g. road, railways, forests, minerals, river valley projects, etc. These national resources are used for the social welfare of man.

(3) International resources : These include all the material and non-material, things of the world. They are used for the benefit of the human race.

Use of Resources

- The economic prosperity of any region, to a large extent, depends on the availability and use of resources. The utility of these things depends on the culture of man, which has grown out of the interaction. Since the dawn of human history, man has utilised the resources to satisfy his needs. He has used trees to produce fire, to collect fruits and nuts, to make clothing of the leaves and to make his dwelling in the hollows of their trunks. Since time immemorial, man has used soil to grow a variety of crops. He has used rivers to irrigate his lands. He has breathed pure air, drunk pure water. He scratched minerals from the earth's crust to make his crude implements and tools.

This problem arises from two factors :

(1) The ever increasing number of people living in the 20th century demands more resources. This large scale demand of resources created a world-wide problem and poses a threat to the very existence of many resources.

(2) Man's developing techniques, growing scientific knowledge and the art of finding out newer uses for resources has revolutionised the rate of exploitation of resources. Man initially used oil as a power resource but soon he came to know its other uses also. Oil serves as lubricant, an illuminant and its by-products are used in the chemical, textile, pharmaceutical and in many other industries. Thus, the rate of exploitation of oil is now on a very large scale.

- Utilization of resources includes both-rational utilization and conservation resources for the maximum benefit of human society. Today we are using resources on a large scale but we have to utilise them in such a way that future generations will also get their benefits.

Resources should be utilised in the following ways :

(1) Man is unable to produce exhaustible resources, e.g. iron and coal, once removed from the earth, cannot be replaced. Such resources, should be replaced by renewable resources, so that these exhaustible resources will be used on a smaller scale. For example, man is able to use hydro-electric power, solar energy, wind energy Instead of coal to run his machinery. He is also able to use green-manure instead of chemical fertilizers to retain the fertility of the soil.

(2) With improved techniques and scientific knowledge, man is able to recycle certain resources. This is one of the methods of conservation of resources. Scrap and worn out machinery can be used as a raw material in the iron and steel industry. Such recycling is essential to increase the longevity of many resources.

(3) The resources should be used in such a way that there will be a minimum wastage. With increasing exploitation and use of resources, the earth is becoming poorer and poorer day by day. Many of the sugar industries use bagasse as a fuel. If these plants use hydroelectricity as a power resource, bagasse will not go waste as a fuel. It can be used to manufacture paper. During 'fall' season, the dry leaves of the trees, may be collected in pits and can be used to make manure.

(4) The rational use of-resources should be supplemented by constant research through which alternative inexhaustible resources can be made available. The highly industrialised nations have to take into consideration the rate of depletion of fossil fuels, e.g. with the present rate of consumption of oil, the total reserves of the world will be exhausted within 30 years. Hence emphasis should be placed on new power resources like solar energy, wind energy and nuclear energy.

(5) It is essential to have correct estimate of a country's resources. This is important in the planning and use of the country's present reserves. For instance, a country with small reserves of coal will give an emphasis to the development of its hydro-electric power. Such a country will produce minimum amount of coal; e.g. Japan. To conserve its home supplies and supplement home production. the U.S.A. imports oil on a large scale. Thus, once the picture of the country's resources is made clear, it is easy to plan their utilization.

(6) In order to lay down the policy of conservation, it is essential to make assessment of future needs. Then it is possible to prepare a suitable budget in accordance with the assessment of ability and needs in the present as well as the future.

(7) The governments of the respective countries should lay down laws regarding the utilization of resources. Such laws and regulations are useful to curb malpractices like robbery, wasteful methods of exploiting resources and will also regulate the use of non-renewable resources. The example of Myanmar is useful in this context. There are pure stands of teak in northern Myanmar. The teak trees were cut to such an extent that these forests were impoverished. Now the country has greatly reduced the output of teak in order to conserve this valuable resource..

(8) The most important factor in the utilization of resources, is the general awareness of people regarding the valuable resource wealth. People should become resource conscious.

- Experiments made in the last three decades have shown that there can be no rational and equitable economic development without environmental conservation. Unless and until people realize the importance of conservation of resources, all laws and statutes of resource conservation are useless. For this purpose, mass education regarding resources is essential so that people will realize the gravity of the present situation.

2.1.3 Importance of Natural Resources

Importance of Natural Resources

- Natural resources maintain a complex interaction between living and non-living things and humans benefit from this interaction.
- People consume resources directly or indirectly globally. Developed countries consume resources more than under-developed countries.
- The world economy uses around 60 billion tonnes of resources each year to produce the goods and services which we all consume globally.
- On an average, a European consumes about 36 kg of resources per day; an individual in North America consumes about 90 kg per day, an Asian consumes about 14 kg and a person in Africa consumes about 10 kg of resources per day.
- People consume natural resources in the form of food and drink, housing and infrastructure, and mobility. They make up more than 60% of resource use.

(i) Food and drink :

- Food includes agricultural products, hunting, fish from fresh water and seas, seeds and nuts, medicines, herbs and plants.
- It includes drinking water, as well as water for sanitation and household use. Never ceramic plates, silverware, cans, milk packages, paper and plastic cups — all are made from raw materials derived from natural resources.

(ii) Mobility (Transportation) :

- Products such as automobiles, trains, water vessels, airplanes, etc. with all the fuel are made from natural resources. All the raw materials used in their production came from natural resources.

(iii) Housing and infrastructure :

- Houses, public places, roads and construction in the cities or town, heating and cooling in the homes, all the wood, metals, plastic, stone and other materials come from natural resources.
- Beyond the above mentioned resource consumption, we consume much more resources from our environment on a daily basis. Natural resources sustain life on earth and we must ensure that we protect the environment and make it more sustainable.

2.2 TYPES OF FORESTS, CHARACTERISTICS, DISTRIBUTION AND SIGNIFICANCE

2.2.1 Forests

A forest is a formation consisting of trees, growing close together and forming a layer of foliage which largely shades the ground. It is an area of wood uncultivated land. Trees require more warmth, moisture and sunlight than any other plants. Normally, the trees require a minimum temperature of 6°C for their growth. However, the intensity and duration of temperature required varies according to the different species of trees. Due to the higher rate of evaporation in tropical areas, trees require a rainfall of more than 75 cm and hence grow in the wetter parts whereas the trees that grow in the temperate areas require a precipitation of over 35 cm as the rate of evaporation is less in these areas. Extreme cold is the reason why forests do not occur in the polar areas and on the upper slopes of the mountains. Again, the absence of adequate moisture inhibits the growth of the trees and hence forests are not found in the arid and semi-arid areas of the world.

Forest :

- A forest can be defined as a large area dominated by trees.
- According Food and Agriculture Organization (FAO) definition, forests covered 4 billion hectares or approximately 30 percent of the world's land area in 2006.
- Forests are the dominant terrestrial ecosystem of earth, and account for 75% of the gross primary production of the earth's biosphere, and consists of 80% of the earth's plant biomass.

- Forests at different latitudes form different ecozones : i.e. boreal forests around the poles, forests around the Equator, and temperate forests at the middle latitudes.
- The amount of precipitation also affects forest composition.
- Forests provide ecosystem services to humans and serve as tourist attractions however it can also affect people's health. Human activities can also negatively affect forest ecosystems.

Definition :

- There are three categories of forest definitions :
(i) Administrative definitions are based primarily upon the legal designations of land, and bear little relationship to the vegetation growing on the land: land that is legally designated as a forest is defined as a forest even if no trees are growing on it.
(ii) Land use definitions are based upon the primary purpose that the land serves. For example, a forest may be defined as any land that is used primarily for production of timber. Under such a land use definition, cleared roads or infrastructure within an area used for forestry, or areas within the region that have been cleared by harvesting, are still considered forests even if they contain no trees.
(iii) Land cover definitions define forests based upon the type and density of vegetation growing on the land.
- An area of land can only be known as forest if it is growing trees. Areas that fail to meet the land cover definition may be still included under which immature trees are establishing if they are expected to meet the definition at maturity.
- The word forest comes from Middle English, from Old French forest (also forès) "forest, vast expanse covered by trees"; first introduced in English as the word for wild land set aside for hunting.
- The first known forests on Earth arose (approximately 380 million years ago, with the evolution of Archaeopteris. Archaeopteris was a plant that was both tree-like and fern-like, growing to 10 metres (33 ft) in height.
- Archaeopteris quickly spread throughout the world, from the equator to subpolar latitudes. Archaeopteris formed the first forest by being the first known species to cast shade due to its fronds and forming soil from its roots. Archaeopteris was deciduous, dropping its fronds onto the forest floor.
- Forests account for 75% of the gross primary productivity of the Earth's biosphere, and contain 80% of the Earth's plant biomass. Forest ecosystems can be found in all regions capable of sustaining tree growth.
- The latitudes 10° north and south of the equator are mostly covered in tropical rainforest, and the latitudes between 53°N and 67°N have boreal forest. As a general rule, forests dominated by angiosperms (broadleaf forests) are more species.
- Forests sometimes contain many tree species within a small area (as in tropical rain and temperate deciduous forests), or relatively few species over large areas (e.g., taiga and arid montane coniferous forests). Forests are often home to many animal and plant species.

- A forest consists of many components that can be broadly divided into two categories that are biotic (living) and abiotic (non-living) components. The living parts include trees, shrubs, vines, grasses and other herbaceous (non-woody) plants, mosses, algae, fungi, insects, mammals, birds, reptiles, amphibians, and microorganisms living on the plants and animals and in the soil.

Layers :

- A forest is made up of many layers. The main layers of all forest types are the forest floor, the understory and the canopy and each layer has a different set of plants and animals depending upon the availability of sunlight, moisture and food.

(i) Forest floor consists of decomposing leaves, animal droppings, and dead trees. Decay on the forest floor forms new soil and provides nutrients to the plants. The forest floor supports ferns, grasses, mushroom and tree seedlings.

(ii) Understory is made up of bushes, shrubs, and young trees that are adapted to living in the shades of the canopy.

(iii) Canopy is formed by the mass of intertwined branches, twigs and leaves of the mature trees, and receive most of the sunlight. This is the most productive part of the trees where maximum food is produced. The canopy forms a shady, protective "umbrella" over the rest of the forest.

- Emergent layer exists in the tropical rain forest and is composed of a few scattered trees that tower over the canopy.

Areas Under Forests

- Only a few centuries back, nearly 60% of the land surface of the Earth was covered by forests. But as a result of the increased population, large forested areas have been cleared in order to make way for agriculture, settlements, industries and arteries of transportation. To-day, only 25% of the land surface of the earth is covered by forests and the distribution, of forest cover is highly uneven.
- The present forest cover is found in two major areas. On the basis of the areas in which forests are found, they are divided into two groups commonly known as :

(1) The Tropical forests : These are found in the tropical areas between 30° N and $23\frac{1}{2}^{\circ}$ S.

(2) The Temperate forests : These are found in the temperate lands between 30° and 70° latitudes in both hemispheres.

- On the basis of the nature of the trees that are found in these forests, they are further into two sub-types.

    (i) Evergreen forests : In these forests, all the trees do not shed their leaves in any one particular season, and therefore, these' forests appear green throughout the year.

    (ii) Deciduous forests : In these forests, all the trees shed their leaves in the season when the moisture is inadequate. In certain tropical areas, there is a distinct dry summer season during which the trees shed their leaves, while in the temperate lands, trees shed their leaves during the very cold season of winter when the ground water is frozen.

Thus, the forests are classified as follows :

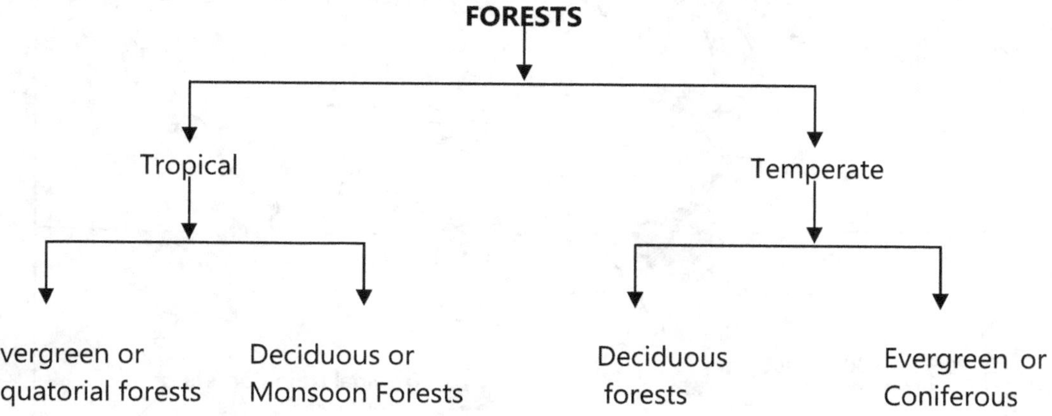

Fig. 2.1

I. **The Equatorial Forests or The Tropical Rain Forests (Map 2.1)**

The climatic conditions under which these forests exist are :

(a) A constant high temperature of around 27°C.

(b) A heavy rainfall of more than 200 cm, evenly distributed throughout the year.

(c) High relative humidity.

Areas under equatorial forests :

- These forests exist roughly between 10°N and 10°S latitudes and are found following areas :

(1) **South America :** A broad stretch of forests is found in the Amazon basin. These forests are locally known as the Sehwas. Excluding the highlands of the Andes, these forests stretch from the Pacific coast to the Atlantic coast. To the north of the equator, these forests extend up to Maxico and to the south of the equator they extend upto the Tropic of Capricorn.

(2) **Africa :** The evergreen forests occur in three main areas :

(a) In the coastal areas of West Africa,

(b) In the Congo Basin (Zaire basin).

(c) In the eastern coastal areas of Africa between 3°N and 10°S latitudes, covering eastern Malagasy.

(3) **South East Asia :** These forests are found in Malaysia, and Indonesia, Papua New Guinea and the coastal lowlands of other South and South East Asian countries.

The major characteristics of The Rain Forests are :

(1) A well distributed conventional rainfall arid a constant high temperature provide optimum conditions for plant growth. The trees grow without any interruption and numerous varieties of trees grow together. Nearly 200 species of different trees grow in one sq. km.

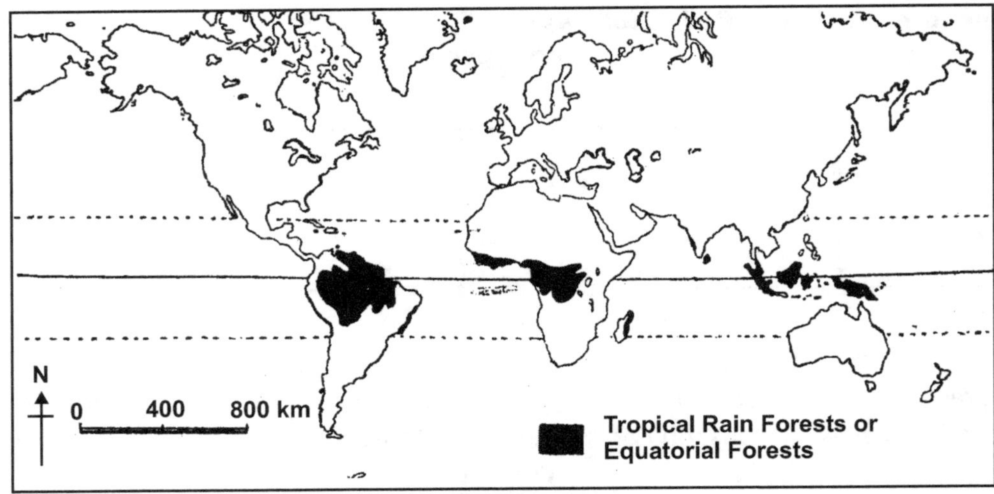

Map 2.1

(2) The trees are mainly broad-leaved and evergreen. Due to lack of dry or cool season the trees do not shed their leaves in any one particular season and hence, these forests appear green throughout the year.

(3) The wood of these trees is hard and thus these trees are commonly referred to as hardwoods. The wood is so hard and heavy that it does not float on water.

(4) As the trees grow close together, there is a keen competition among them for sunlight. Hence, these forests are, made up of three tiers or layers. The highest layer is made up of trees that grow upto a height of 46 m. Beneath these tall trees are the trees that grow upto 18 meters which form the second tier. The lowest layer is made up of smaller trees which grow up to 15 meters (Diag. 2.2)

Fig. 2.2

(5) Trees do not have branches in the lower two-thirds /of their trunks'. The branches appear in the upper one-third. The trunks of these trees are straight and are supported by buttressed roots which give a firm support to the trees. These roots are like walls and radiate in different directions. (Diagram 2.3). The long straight trunks are ideal for timber and for construction.

Diag. 2.3   **Diag. 2.4**

(6) Numerous epiphytes, parasites and lianas grow in the forest. Epiphytes like orchids and ferns use other plants for support. The parasitic plants get their food from plants. Lanes or woody climbers girdle the trees and hang down in great loops (Diagram 2.4).

(7) The commercially important trees are rubber, green heart, logwood, acapu, ivory wood, ebony, mahogany, satinwood, oil palm and iron wood.

Problems associated with the Equatorial forests

(1) Excluding South-East Asia, these forests cover large, compact areas in South America and Africa and hence are impenetrable.

(2) They are found in areas which experience an inhospitable climate. The climate is hot and humid in which the spread of diseases like malaria, yellow fever and sleeping sickness is quite common. Thus, the region is sparsely populated and there is a shortage of efficient labour.

(3) Numerous species of trees grow close together and to locate and extract the valuable trees becomes difficult.

(4) Though the hardwoods are valuable, their exploitation is difficult due to inadequate transportation facilities. It is not only difficult to fell the hardwoods and construct roads and railways, but their maintenance is very costly because under hot and humid climatic conditions, the vegetation cover quickly encroaches on the tracks.

(5) The hardwood trees of the equatorial forests cannot be utilized for making paper and pulp which has an ever-increasing demand in the market. With the introduction of iron-steel and cement in the field construction, the hardwoods have lost their previous importance.

(6) Many tribal people in the equatorial forests practise shifting agriculture by burning the valuable forests. Once the tree cover has been destroyed, the rate of soil erosion accelerates due to heavy rainfall. The original varieties of trees are unable to establish themselves in the poor soil. Thus each year, the areas under valuable forests are diminishing.

(7) Since the equatorial forests are sparsely populated, there is no large local demand for timber. Thus, the major market which lies in the western countries is far away.

II. Tropical Deciduous or Monsoon Forests

• These forests occur under the following climatic conditions :

(1) The total rainfall varies between 100 and 250 cm, but occur mainly during summer.

(2) A distinct long dry season in which there is shortage of moisture.

Areas under the tropical deciduous, forests (Map 2.2)

- These forests originally covered large areas of India, Bangladesh, Myanmar, Thailand, Laos, Kampuchea and Vietnam. But due to human interference over a long period, the plateaus and the plains are comparatively devoid of forests.

- Due to tremendous pressure of population on the land, the original forest cover has been removed over large areas and hence, today, it is found mainly in the remote hilly and mountainous areas of these countries.

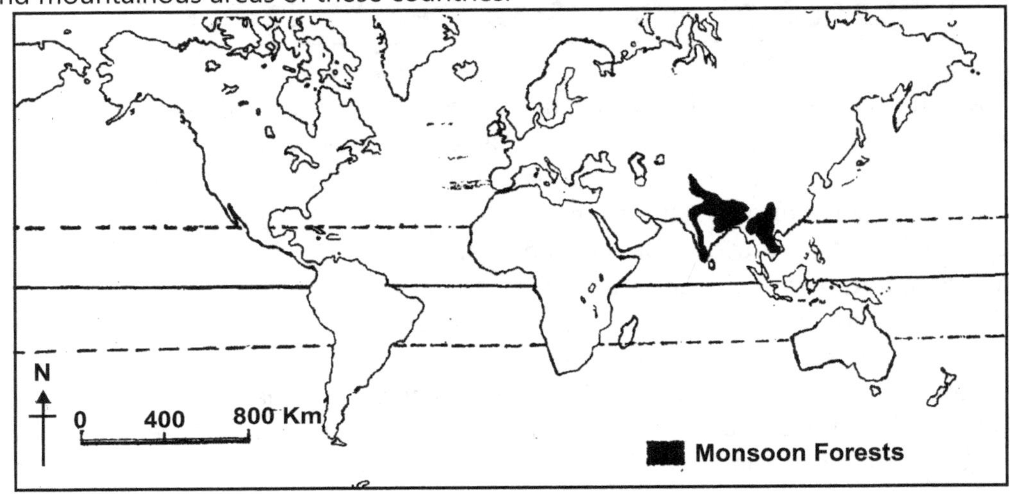

Map. 2.2

The major characteristics of the Monsoon forests

(1) Large variations in the trees are found depending on the total annual rainfall. The trees vary from the evergreen trees of the wetter areas to the Savanna woodland of the drier areas.

(2) The trees are hardwoods. They shed their leaves at the beginning of the dry period and burst into flowers and leaves at the onset of rainy season.

(3) This forest is not very dense as compared to the equatorial evergreen forest. It is more open. But a dense undergrowth and bamboo clumps are found.

(4) All the trees are not very tall and only some grow up to 30 metres. The three tier system is also found in these forest.

(5) The commercially important trees are teak, sal, banyan, sandalwood, acacias and ironwood.

(6) Bamboo, which occurs in thickets is found on a large scale. Nearly 300 varieties of bamboo are found in the Monsoon forests of Asia.

(7) Woody lianas, parasites and epiphytes are almost absent.

Lumbering :

- Lumbering is a difficult task because the monsoon forests lie mainly in the remote highland areas where roads and railways are inadequate.

Problems :

(1) The Monsoon forests now occur only in remote highlands away from the densely populated areas.

(2) These areas do not have adequate transportation facilities. Thus transportation of logs is carried on with the help of elephants which is a costly and time-consuming process. The rivers are used to carry logs. A floating log in the Irrawaddy river takes one full year to reach the port of Rangoon from the northern hilly areas.

(3) The forests do not occur in pure stands and hence exploitation of commercially important trees becomes difficult.

(4) The tribal people of the mountainous areas burn patches of forest to bring the land under shifting cultivation. Thus, the area covered by valuable trees is decreasing.

(II) The Temperate Deciduous Hardwood Forests

The climatic conditions under which these tree grow :

(1) Moderate temperatures : Summers are not very hot but winters are very cold.

(2) Moderate rainfall : 75 to 150 cm which is evenly distributed throughout the year.

Areas under the Temperate Deciduou Forests (Map 2.3)

• These forests are found between 30° and 50° latitudes in both hemispheres. Once they covered large areas of China, Japan, West, South and Central Europe as well as large parts of Eastern North America and also in Tasmania and Swanland in Australia. Due to the growth of industries and the expansion of agriculture, large forested areas have been reduced in their extent and are found only in remote areas.

Major characteristics of temperate, deciduous forests

(1) Numerous species of trees grow in these forests. The forest does not occur in pure stands.

(2) Though the forest is not dense, there is a heavy undergrowth.

(3) Majority of the trees are broad-leaved and hardwoods and shed their leaves before winter. When temperature is below freezing point, the trees are unable to absorb moisture from the frozen soil. The trees remain leafless throughout the winter to conserve the moisture and the forest appears lifeless.

(4) Most deciduous trees have a thick, tough bark as a protection against frost.

(5) The trees are not very tall and rarely attain height of 30 m.

(6) The chief commercial species are the oak, birch, poplar, ash, chestnut, elm and walnut.

Activities associated with the temperate hard wood forests

• People from these areas have now realised the importance of this natural valuable resources. The Government takes a keen interest and in many areas of Europe, where soil is unsuitable for agriculture, trees have been planted. Many of these forests are owned by the government and are protected. Hence. forestry is not an important commercial activity.

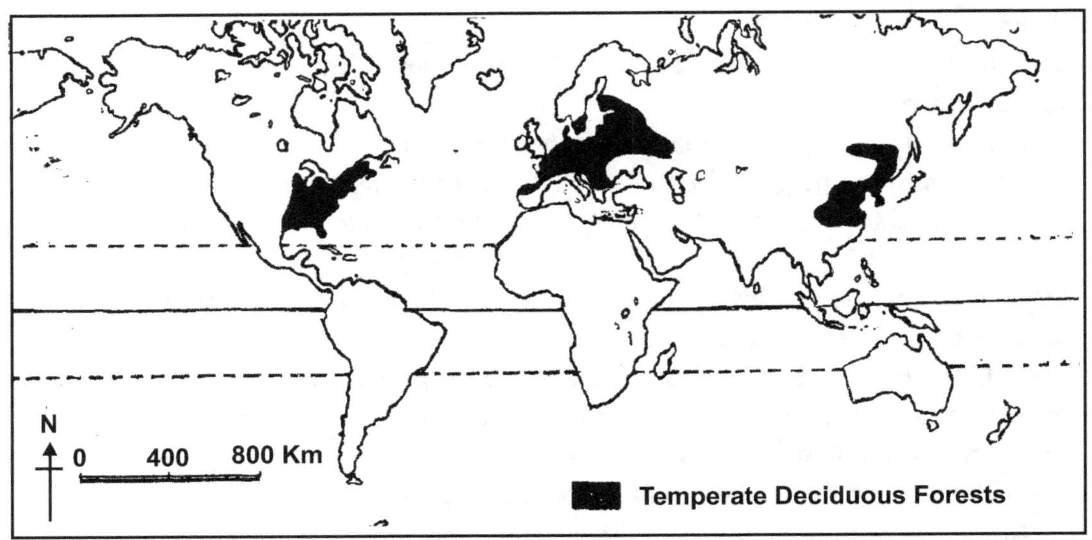

Fig. 2.3

(IV) Temperate Softwood or Coniferous Forests

These forests are commonly known as the Boreal or Taiga forests.

Climatic conditions under which these forests grow

(1) Summers are warm and short with temperatures above 6°C.

(2) Winters are long and very cold and temperature remains below freezing point.

(3) Precipitation is moderate and varies between 30 and 76 cm. It occurs mainly in summer, but snow falls in winter.

Areas under the Coniferous Forests (Map 2.4)

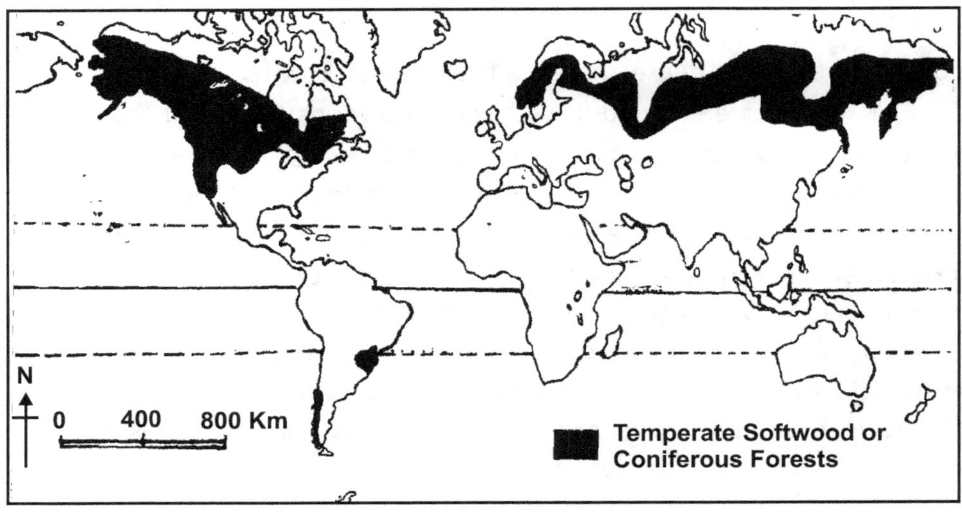

Map 2.4

- These forests occur between 50° and 70° latitudes in both hemispheres. Due to the large extent of the landmasses in between these latitudes in the northern hemisphere. these forests occur in a wide and large belt. As the land mass between these latitudes in southern hemisphere is small, the coniferous forests are found in small areas.

(1) Eurasia : These forests occur over a long stretch of about 8,030 km from the Atlantic coast of Norway to the Pacific coasts of eastern Russian Federation, Norway, Sweden, Finland and the European part of the Russian Federation have large areas of soft woods. Due to vast swampy and marshy areas, these forests are not continuous in the Asiatic part of the Russian Federation. These forests become thin towards the north due to cold climate, and towards the south because of dry climate.

(2) North America : Along the west coast of North America, the climate is moist, and hence, the forest is thick in the states of California, Washington and Oregon in the U. S. A. and in Western Canada. This belt continues towards the east, but the forest is not so thick in the central and eastern parts due to dry climate and poor soil. Conifers also occur in southern parts of the U. S. A., from Virginia to Texas.

(3) South America : Coniferous forests occur in small areas of the southern Brazilian plateau and the coastal areas of southern Chile.

Major characteristics of the Coniferous forests

(1) With the exception of the larch, the coniferous trees are evergreen and are well adapted to the severe climatic conditions. They have needle shaped leaves which reduce the water loss by transpiration, they have thick barks to protect them from frost and are conical in shape which helps to shed snow and face the strong winds. They bear their seeds in cones which do not rot so easily. The trees are named after these cones and are known as conifers.

(2) The trees grow upto a height of 30 metres and their trunks are tall and straight. Their wood is soft and hence the forests are referred to as softwood forests. The wood is easily turned into pulp which is used in making paper and synthetic fibres.

(3) The forests are thick in areas where the climate is moist, e.g. in the western coastal areas of North America. Otherwise, they are moderately thick and become thin in the cold and dry areas.

(4) The most important peculiarity of this forest is "that it occurs in pure stands, i. e. one type of tree grows over a large area. Due to this distinct characteristic, lumbering on large scale commercial basis is possible.

(5) The undergrowth is usually sparse and is found in the form of shrubs, mosses and lichens.

(6) The major species of trees are the varieties of spruces, pines and firs. Deciduous trees like birches and larches also found in these forests are.

Activities associated with the temperate softwood Forests :

- The activity of lumbering is more important in these forests than the gathering of forest products. In many temperate countries. lumbering is practised on a commercial scale and the wood and wood pulp is exported on a large scale.

(I) Lumbering :

- Various factors have made large scale lumbering possible in these forests :

(1) The nature of the forests : The forests occur in 'pure stands'. If the trees are important, the easiest method of extraction is used. This method is known as "clear felling" in which all the trees in one area are cut. This saves time and cuts down the cost.

(2) The nature of trees : The trees in the coniferous forests are not as tall, or as hard as the tropical trees. They are short, light and their wood is soft. Unlike the equatorial trees, they do not have buttress roots. Lumber jacks can cut the trees at ground level. Thus, lumbering is easy.

(3) Very cold and long winters : Snowfalls during winter and the ground is covered with snow. Even the rivers are frozen during this period. The logs are easily dragged over frozen rivers tied into rafts. The snow melts in spring and summer and the logs are floated downstream, directly to the sawmills which are located near the river banks. Thus, the climate favours easy and cheap transportation of logs.

(4) Nearness to the market : Excluding the coniferous forests of South America and Siberia, the coniferous forests of North America and Europe are very close to the markets.

- The major markets for the forest products lie in Europe and the U, S. A. These densely populated and industrialised areas create an ever-increasing market for the forest products. Thus, the cost of transportation is low.

(5) A large demand for the softwoods' : The softwood of the coniferous trees can be easily turned into pulp which contains cellulose. This pulp is used in making paper and synthetic fibres like nylon and rayon. Both these products have an increasing demand all over the world. Traditionally, softwood is also used for making furniture and for constructional purposes. The lumber jack of these forests live in log cabins which remain during winter.

(6) Renewed forest resources : In Canada, the U. S. A. and the European countries their respective Governments take parental care-of the forests to see that wasteful methods of lumbering are not practiced. After clearing a forested strip, new saplings are immediately planted and they are well looked after. Lumbering is practised on a rotational basis and replanted areas are again cleared after a period of about 70 years, when the trees are ready to cut.

- In many marginal northern parts of Sweden, Norway and Finland, the cold climate does not permit the cultivation of crops. The Government encourages the farmers of these areas to grow trees instead of growing crops because the trees yield a higher income. Thus, large areas have been brought under forests in these countries. Due to these favourable factors, lumbering is practiced on a large scale in Canada, the Russian Federation and U. S. A., Norway, Sweden and Finland.

Use of Forests

The Equatorial Forests

- The forests have hardwood trees but due to inadequate transportation facilities, valuable timber is extracted from accessible areas of forests. Such areas lie near the rivers and coasts. Mahogany and ironwood are the most valuable trees as their wood is hard and durable. It is used for constructional purposes.

- Various useful parts of the hardwood trees are collected; e.g. roots, barks, leaves, nuts, flowers, fruits, gum, etc. They are collected by native people. Many of these products have a large demand in the western market. Chickle is used for making the popular chewing gum; balata is used for making undersea cables and golf ball covers; ivory nuts are used for making buttons. Quinine is obtained from the bark of the chichona tree. Fruits, fresh nuts and leaves are consumed locally.

The Monsoon Forests

- As areas under these forests are small, lumbering in these areas is practised on a limited scale.
- The wood of the deciduous trees is very hard and is useful for construction, furniture, etc. Teak is an important tree in Assam in India, Myanmar, Thailand and Kampuchea. Sandalwood is derived from the Nilgiri hills and the adjacent highlands. The scented wood is used in the handicraft industries, in which, a variety of carved articles are made. Bamboo is used in construction and for making paper.
- Like the equatorial forests, a large variety of products is collected from Monsoon forests. Among them oilseeds, mahua seed is very important. These seeds are collected from the forests of Madhya Pradesh in India. Lac is produced mostly in the forests of Chota Nagpur region.
- The tanning material is obtained from the babul (acacia) tree. Tannin is used in the leather industry in order to make hides durable, flexible and strong. The leaves of tendu trees in India are used for making bidis. A large variety of medicinal herbs are collected.

(V) The Temperate Evergreen (Coniferous) Forests

- The trees in these forests are softwoods. The softwood can be easily turned into pulp which contains cellulose. This pulp is used in making paper and synthetic fibres like nylon and rayon. Both these products have an increasing demand in the world market. Traditionally, softwood is also used for making furniture and for constructional purposes.
- From commercial point of view, these are the most valuable and useful forests. Canada, the U. S. A., Norway, Sweden, Finland and Germany produce pulp, paper and newsprint which is used by the entire world.
- Besides these commercial uses, the forests play a very important role in our environment. They have various functions to perform. These functions are of three broad categories-protective, productive and recreational. The following are some of the major uses of forests from environmental point of view -

(1) The forests check the rate of soil erosion. The leaves, branches of the trees act as a buffer against the force of the rain, which then gently falls to the ground. Thus the soil is protected from the direct impact of raindrops, otherwise the soil particles become loose and are easily washed away by rainwater.

(2) Due to the trees, rainwater gets a chance to sink into the soil which is kept porous by rootholes and by the presence of organic matter. The water so retained flows

underground by the force of gravity and comes out as springs which keep the rivers alive long after the rains are over.

(3) The forests influence the temperature of air. In the cold regions forests prevent radiation of heat and keep up the temperature and the hot regions they help to lower the temperature of the locality by casting their heavy shade.

(4) The forests help in increasing the rainfall of a region as more moisture is added from the transpiration of the leaves and temperature is lowered by the canopy of the trees.

(5) The Forests act as wind breakers and thereby check the ravages of storms. The trees in the large tropical plantations prove extremely beneficial to check the strong winds. They also prevent the movement of soil by the action of wind. Along the coast the inward movement of sand is checked by planting the sands with Casuarina trees. Thus the trees can prevent the shifting of sand dunes.

(6) The forests check the rate of soil 41 erosion binding soil with their roots. On the mountain slopes, forest cover is beneficial to check the landslides and to check the rate of run-off. Rainwater, instead of flowing unchecked, enters in the soil. Thus the forests check the severity of floods.

(7) Forests are the homes of varied wild-life.

(8) The recreational value of forests is also very important. They are the areas of scenic beauty and ideal places of relaxation and recuperation from the tension, strain and impure atmosphere of cities and towns. They attract the youth for adventure.

- We can summarise the importance of forests in the words of great American architect, Frank Lloyd Wright, "Wood is a friend of mine. The best friend of earth, of man, is the tree. When we use the trees respectfully and economically, we have one of the greatest resources of the earth. If a man is going to live, he should live with wood."

2.2.2 Societal Significance :

Diversity of ecosystem services provided by Forests include :

- Trees convert carbon dioxide into oxygen and biomass and a full-grown tree produces about 100 kg of net oxygen per year.

- Acting as a carbon sink so they are necessary to stop climate change. According to a Special Report in order to avoid temperature rise by more than 1.5 degrees above pre-industrial levels, there will need to be an increase in global forest cover equal to the land by 10 million km^2, by the year 2050.

- Aiding in regulating climate. For example, a research from 2017, show that forests induce rainfall. If the forest is cut, it can lead to drought.

(i) Purifying water.

(ii) Mitigating natural hazards such as floods.

(iii) Serving as a genetic reserve.

(iv) Serving as a source of lumber and as recreational areas.

- Some researchers state that forests do not only provide benefits, but can in certain cases also incur costs to humans.

- The management of forests is often referred to as forestry. Forest management has changed culminating in a practice now referred to as sustainable forest management.
- Humans have generally decreased the amount of forest available due to worldwide anthropogenic logging, urban sprawl, human-caused forest fires, acid rain, invasive species, and the slash and burn practices of shifting cultivation.
- In 1997, a study recorded that only 20% of the world's original forests remained in large intact tracts of undisturbed forest and 75% of these intact forests lie in three countries— the boreal forests of Russia and Canada and the rainforest of Brazil.
- In 2010, FAO reported that world deforestation, the conversion of tropical forests to agricultural land, still continues at a high rate in many countries. Globally, around 13 million hectares of forests were converted to other uses or lost through natural causes each year between 2000 and 2010 (covered 233 countries).
- Brazil and Indonesia, which had the highest loss of forests have significantly reduced their deforestation rates. China instituted a ban on logging, due to the erosion and flooding that it caused.
- A study for Nature Climate Change showed that the trend has recently been reversed, leading to an "overall gain" in global biomass and forests. a 2015, the Food and FAO of the United Nations released a new study stating that, over the last 25 years, the global deforestation rate has decreased by 50% due to improved management of forests and government protection.

2.2.3 Importance of Forests

- Such is the importance of forests that we depend on forests for our survival, from the air we breathe to the wood we use. Forests provide habitats for animals and livelihoods for human, offers watershed protection, prevents soil erosion and mitigate climate change.
- Forests give us shelter, livelihoods, water, food and fuel security. All these activities directly or indirectly involve forests. i.e. fruits, paper and wood from trees, etc. including by-products such as medicines, cosmetics and detergents.
- Forests are home to 80% of the world's terrestrial biodiversity, and they also form the source of livelihood for many humans.
- Millions of people live in forests, including 60 million indigenous people.
- When we destroy the forests, it is not just the trees that go it is the entire ecosystem which falls apart, with serious consequences for humans.
- Next to oceans, forests are the world's largest storehouses of carbon.
- In summary they provide ecosystem services that are critical to human welfare which are as follows :
(a) Providing clean water for drinking, bathing, and other household needs.
(b) Absorbing harmful greenhouse gasses that produce climate change. In tropical forests alone, a quarter of a trillion tons of carbon is store in above and below ground biomass.
(c) Protecting watershed and reducing or slowing the amount of erosoin and chemicals that reach waterways.

(d) Providing food and medicine.

(e) Providing habitat to more that half of the world's land-based species.

(f) Serving as a buffer in natural disasters like flood and rainfalls

2.3 NON-CONVENTIONAL ENERGY RESOURCES - SOLAR, WIND AND TIDAL ENERGY

Non-Conventional Energy Resources :

- The energy crisis experienced during the seventh decade of the last century forced the scientists to develop alternative sources of energy which are renewable and which may be used for longer period of time. Mineral oil and coal are exhaustible. The scientists have introduced non-conventional energy resources like sun, wind, wave and geothermal energy.

Non-Conventional Sources :

- Natural resources like wind, tides, solar, biomass, etc generate energy which is known as **"Non-conventional resources"**. These are pollution free and hence we can use these to produce a clean form of energy without any wastage.

Need for non-conventional energy resources :

- As the consumption of energy grows, the population has started depending more and more on fossil fuels such as coal, oil and gas. There is a need to secure the energy supply for future since the prices of gas and oil keep increasing by each passing day. So the need increasing for more and more renewable sources of energy.

- For the effective exploitation of non-conventional sources, there is a separate department called "Department of non-conventional sources of energy" of government of India.

Renewable resources provide energy in four important areas :

- Electricity generation
- Water heating or cooling
- Transporting
- Rural

Types of Non-convention sources

- Solar Energy
- Wind Energy
- Tidal Energy
- Geothermal Energy
- Biomass

2.3.1 Solar Energy

Solar Energy :

- Energy derived from the sun is known as solar energy. The tropical and sub-tropical areas get abundant sunlight which can be utilised as a power resource.

- Solar system is used in two ways. In the first, plates are used to collect and reflect the heat and in the other photo voltaic cells are used to convert light into electric current.
- Solar collectors collect solar energy in the form of heat. The black surface of the solar collectors helps to convert sunlight into heat. A copper coil pipe on the black metal surface carries water. With the heat, water in the pipe gets hot. This hot water can be used to heat the buildings or for bathing or washing.
- Photo voltaic cells which are composed of semi-conducting material convert light into electric current. Solar cells are used in watches, cameras and calculators. Spacecrafts also use solar energy. Today several countries of the world are manufacturing solar cells on the commercial scale. The U.S.A. is the largest producer of solar cells. Japan, France, Italy, Germany, Australia, Belgium, Brazil, Canada, China, India, Mexico, the, U.K., Russian Federation and Spain also produce photo voltaic cells.
- Solar energy may play an important role in rural electrification. It will be also available for pumping water, refrigeration and irrigation. Several research institutions in India have initiated major programme for solar energy utilisation in water heating, grain drying, food preservation, pumping, power generation, etc. Considerable progress has already been achieved in solar thermal extension programme, e.g. (a) Sale of 2 lakh solar cookers, (b) setting up of 10,000 street lighting systems in villages using photo-voltaic technology.
- Solar energy may prove to be an important source of energy in the future but it has some drawbacks. Solar energy is useless in areas where there is a dense and continuous cloud cover. It also cannot be utilised in poleward areas of the temperate lands and polar areas due to low intensity of insolation.
- Like hydro-electric power, solar energy is also an inexhaustible source of energy Moreover, its importance lies in the fact that it is non-air-pollutant.
- Solar energy collects heat from the Sun that is captured using technologies such as solar heating, photo voltaics, solar thermal energy, solar architecture, molten salt power plants and artificial photosynthesis.
- Its technologies are broadly characterized as either passive solar or active solar depending on how they capture and distribute solar energy or convert it into solar power.
- The large amount of solar energy available makes it a demanded source of electricity.
- 174 petawatts (PW) of solar radiation (insolation) at the and approximately 30% is reflected back to space while the rest is.

Limitations :
- Factors such as geography, time variation, cloud cover, and the land available to humans restrict the amount of solar energy that we can get.
- Areas that are closer to the equator have a greater amount of solar radiation. The use of photovoltaic that can follow Sun can significantly increase the solar energy potential in areas that are farther from the equator. Time variation effects the potential of solar energy because during the nighttime there is no solar radiation on the surface of the earth for solar panels to absorb.

- Cloud cover can affect the potential of solar panels because clouds block incoming light from the Sun and reduce the light available for solar cells.
- Solar panels can only be set up on land that is otherwise unused and suitable for solar panels.
- Roofs have been found to be a suitable place for solar cells, as many people have discovered that they can collect energy directly from their homes this way.
- Although solar energy refers primarily to the use of solar radiation for practical ends, all renewable energies, other than Geothermal power and Tidal power, get their energy either directly or indirectly from the Sun.
- Active solar technologies increase the supply of energy and are considered supply side technologies, while passive solar technologies reduce the need for alternate resources and are generally considered demand side technologies.
- An estimate of UN found that solar energy has a global potential of 1,600 to 49,800 exajoules (4.4×1014 to 1.4×1016 kWh) per year.

Annual solar energy potential by Solar power in India
- India's solar installed capacity reached 31.696 GW as of 31 October 2019.
- The Indian government had an initial target of 20 GW capacity for 2022, which was achieved four years ahead of schedule.
- India has established 42 solar parks to make land available to the promoters of solar plants.
- India expanded its solar-generation capacity 8 times from 2,650 MW on 26 May 2014 to over 20 GW as on 31 January 2018.
- By the end of 2019, India has installed more than 82,580 MW of renewable energy capacity with around 31,150 MW of capacity under various stages of installation.
- Rooftop solar power accounts for 2.1 GW, of which 70% is industrial or commercial. In addition to its large-scale grid-connected solar photovoltaic (PV) initiative, India is developing off-grid solar power for local energy needs.
- Solar products have increasingly helped to meet rural needs;
- Solar Lanterns were sold in the country, reducing the need for kerosene. That year, 118,700 solar home lighting systems were installed and solar street lighting installations were provided, solar cookers were distributed in India.
- The International Solar Alliance (ISA), proposed by India as a founder member, has headquarts in India.

Installations region :

Table : 2.1 Installated cumulative national and state-wise capacity

Installed solar PV on 31 March	
Year	**Cumulative Capacity (in MW)**
2010	161
2011	461
2012	1,205

Year	Cumulative Capacity (in MW)
2013	2,319
2014	2,632
2015	3,744
2016	6,763
2017	12,289
2018	21,651
2019	28,181

(i) Andhra Pradesh :
- Installed photo-voltaic capacity in Andhra Pradesh become 3,231 MW as on 31st October 2019.
- APGENCO commissioned 400 MW Ananthapuram - II solar park located at Talaricheruvu village near Tadipatri.

(ii) Delhi :
- Delhi is leading in rooftop solar PV installations. The installed solar power capacity is 106 MW as on 30 September 2018.

(iii) Gujarat :
- This state is one of India's most solar-developed states, with its total photovoltaic capacity achieving 1,637 MW by the January 2019. Gujarat has been a leader in solar-power generation due to its high solar-power potential, availability of vacant land, connectivity, transmission and distribution infrastructure and utilities.
- Gujarat has commissioned Asia's largest solar park near the village of Charanka in Patan district.
- In order to make Gandhinagar a solar-power city, the state government has begun a rooftop solar-power generation scheme.
- Gujarat also plans to generate solar power by putting solar panels along the Narmada canals.

(iv) Haryana :
- Haryana has set the 4.2 GW solar power (including 1.6 GW solar roof top) target by 2022 as it has high potential since it has at least 330 sunny days.
- Haryana is one of the fastest growing states in solar energy with installed and commissioned capacity of 73.27 MW.

(v) Karnataka :
- Karnataka is the top solar state in India exceeding 5,000 MW installed capacity by the end of financial year 2017–18.

(vi) Kerala :
- Kerala's has the largest floating solar power plant was established upon the Banasura Sagar Dam reservoir in Wayanad district, Kerala.
- This solar plant has 1,938 solar panels which has been installed.

(vii) Ladakh :
- Ladakh, is planning to install nearly 7,500 MW capacity in the coming years.

(viii) Madhya Pradesh :
- Madhya Pradesh is one of India's most solar-developed states, with its total photovoltaic capacity reaching 1,117 MW by the end of July 2017.
- A 130 MW solar power plant project at Bhagwanpura, a village in Neemuch district, was launched. It is the largest solar producer, and Welspun Energy is one of the top three companies in India's renewable-energy sector.
- A planned 750 MW solar-power plant in Rewa district, the Rewa Ultra Mega Solar, is also planned.

(ix) Maharashtra :
- The 125-MW Sakri solar plant is the largest solar-power plant in Maharashtra. The Shri Saibaba Sansthan Trust has the world's largest solar steam system.
- The total power capacity of Maharashtra is about 500 MW.

(x) Rajasthan :
- Rajasthan is also one of India's most solar-developed states, with its total photovoltaic capacity reaching 2289 MW by end of June 2018. Rajasthan is also home to the worlds largest Fresnel type 125 MW CSP plant at the Dhirubhai Ambani Solar Park.
- The Bhadla Solar Park, is being developed in four phases of which 260 MW capacity was commissioned by NTPC Limited.
- In September 2018 Acme Solar announced that it had commissioned India's cheapest solar power, 200 MW at Bhadla.
- The only tower type solar thermal power plant (2.5 MW) in India is located in Bikaner.

(xi) Tamil Nadu :
- The total operating capacity in Tamil Nadu is 1,8 GW. On 1 July 2017.
- The 648-MW Kamuthi Solar Power Project is the biggest operating project in the state.

(xii) Telangana :
- Telangana ranks second in India when it comes to solar energy generation capacity.
- As of July 2019 by far the largest segment of solar PV installed in India was ground mounted at 27,930 MW installed capacity.

Major photovoltaic power stations
Below is a list of solar power generation facilities with a capacity of at least 10 MW.

Table : 2.2 Major photovoltaic (PV) power plants

Plant	State	DC peak power (MW)	Commissioned
Pavagada Solar Park	Karnataka	1400	March 2019
Kamuthi Solar Power Project	Tamil Nadu	648	21 September 2016
Gujarat Solar Park-1	Gujarat	221	April 2012
Welspun Solar MP project	Madhya Pradesh	151	February 2014
ReNew Power, Nizamabad	Telangana	143	15 April 2017
Sakri solar plant	Maharashtra	125	March 2013
NTPC solar plants		110	2015
Maharashtra I	Maharashtra	67	2017

Plant	State	DC peak power (MW)	Commissioned
Green Energy Development Corporation (GEDCOL)	Odisha	50	2014
Tata Power Solar Systems (TPS), Rajgarh	Madhya Pradesh	50	March 2014
Welspun Energy, Phalodhi	Rajasthan	50	March 2013
Jalaun Solar Power Project	Uttar Pradesh	50	27 January 2016
GEDCOL	Odisha	48	2014
Karnataka I	Karnataka	40	2018
Bitta Solar Power Plant	Gujarat	40	January 2012
Dhirubhai Ambani Solar Park, Pokhran	Rajasthan	40	April 2012
Rajasthan Photovoltaic Plant	Rajasthan	35	February 2013
Welspun, Bathinda	Punjab	34	August 2015
Moser Baer, Patan district	Gujarat	30	October 2011
Lalitpur Solar Power Project	Uttar Pradesh	30	2015
Mithapur Solar Power Plant	Gujarat	25	25 January 2012
GEDCOL	Odisha	20	2014
Kadodiya Solar Park	Madhya Pradesh	15	2014
Telangana I	Telangana	12	2016
Telangana II	Telangana	12	2016
NTPC	Odisha	10	2014
Sunark Solar	Odisha	10	2011
RNS Infrastructure Limited, Pavagada	Karnataka	10	2016
Bolangir Solar Power Project	Odisha	10	2011
Azure Power, Sabarkantha	Gujarat	10	June 2011
Green Infra Solar Energy, Rajkot	Gujarat	10	November 2011
Waa Solar Power Plant, Surendranagar	Gujarat	10	December 2011
Sharda Construction, Latur	Maharashtra	10	June 2015
Ushodaya Project, Midjil	Telangana	10	December 2013

- India's solar capacity reached 19.7 GW by the end of 2017, making it the third-largest global solar market.
- The installed capacity of commercial solar thermal power plants in India is 227.5 MW with 50 MW in Andhra Pradesh and 177.5 MW in Rajasthan.
- Solar-power plants can be installed near existing hydropower and pumped-storage hydroelectricity, utilizing the existing power transmission infrastructure and storing the surplus secondary power generated by the solar PV plants.

- At present concentrated solar thermal installation base for heating applications is about 20 MWth in India and expected to grow rapidly. Cogeneration of steam and power round the clock is also feasible with solar thermal CHP plants with thermal storage capacity.
- Bengaluru has the largest deployment of roof-top solar water heaters in India, generating an energy equivalent of 200 MW.
- An objective of electrifying 5,000 such villages was set for the 2002–2007 Five-Year Plan. By 2004 more than 2,700 villages and hamlets were electrified, primarily with solar photovoltaic systems.
- By 2012, a total of 4,600,000 solar lanterns and 861,654 solar-powered home lights were installed.
- Solar photovoltaic water-pumping systems are used for irrigation and drinking water.
- Solar panels can also be used for harvesting most of the rainwater falling on them and drinking or breweries water quality, free from bacteria and suspended matter, can be generated by simple filtration and disinfection processes, as rainwater is very low in salinity.
- Maximum solar-electricity generation during the hot hours of the day can be used for meeting residential air-conditioning requirements regardless of other load requirements, such as refrigeration, lighting, cooking and water pumping.
- The land price is expensive for acquisition in India.
- The amount of land required for utility-scale solar power plants is about $1km^2$ (250 acres) for every 40–60 MW generated.
- In January 2019, Indian Railways announced the plan to install 4 GW capacity along its tracks.
- The architecture best suited to most of India would be a set of rooftop power-generation systems connected via a local grid.
- Greenpeace recommends that India adopt a policy of developing solar power as a dominant component of its renewable-energy mix, since its identity as a densely-populated country in the tropical belt of the subcontinent has an ideal combination of high insolationand a large potential consumer base.
- Fifty-one solar radiation resource assessment stations have been installed across India by the Ministry of New and Renewable Energy (MNRE) to create a database of solar-energy potential.
- The Indian government is promoting solar energy. It announced an allocation of 1,000 crore for the Jawaharlal Nehru National Solar Mission and a clean-energy fund for the 2010-11 fiscal year, an increase of 380 crore (US$55 million) from the previous budget.
- In January 2016, Prime Minister Narendra Modi and French President François Hollande laid the foundation stone for the headquarters of the International Solar Alliance (ISA) in Gwal Pahari, Gurgaon.

- The 2018 manufacturing capacity of solar cells and solar modules in India was 1,590 MW and 5,620 MW, respectively.
- Indian manufacturers are gradually enhancing the production capacity of monocrystalline silicon PERC cells to supply better performing and enduring solar cells to local market.

2.3.2 Thermal Energy

- Solar thermal technologies can be used for water heating, space heating, space cooling and process heat generation.

(i) Water heating :

- Solar hot water systems use sunlight to heat water. In low geographical latitudes such as below 40 degrees from 60 to 70% of the domestic hot water use with temperatures up to 60 °C can be provided by solar heating systems.
- China is the world leader with 70 GWth installed as of 2006 and a long-term goal of 210 GWth by 2020.
- Israel and Cyprus are the per capita leaders in the use of solar hot water systems with over 90% of homes using them.
- In the United States, Canada, and Australia, heating swimming pools is the dominant application of solar hot water with an installed capacity of 18 GWth as of 2005.

(ii) Heating, cooling and ventilation :

- In the U.S., heating, ventilation and air conditioning systems account for 30% of the energy used in commercial buildings and nearly 50% of the energy used in residential buildings.
- Thermal mass refers to any material that can be used to store heat—heat from the Sun in the case of solar energy. Common thermal mass materials include stone, cement and water.
- A solar chimney is a passive solar ventilation system composed of a vertical shaft connecting the interior and exterior of a building.
- Deciduous trees and plants are means of controlling solar heating and cooling.

(iv) Cooking :

- Solar cookers use sunlight for cooking, drying and pasteurization. They can be grouped into three broad categories: box cookers, panel cookers and reflector cookers.

(v) Process heat :

- Solar concentrating technologies such as parabolic dish, trough and Scheffler reflectors can provide process heat for commercial and industrial applications.

(vi) Water treatment :

- Solar distillation can be used to make saline or brackish water potable.

(vii) Molten salt technology :

- Molten salt can be used as a thermal energy storage method to retain thermal energy collected by a solar tower or solar trough of a concentrated solar power plant, so that it can be used to generate electricity in bad weather or at night.

(viii) Electricity production

- Solar power is the conversion of sunlight into electricity, either directly using photovoltaic (PV), or indirectly using concentrated solar power (CSP). CSP systems use lenses or mirrors and tracking systems to focus a large area of sunlight into a small beam. PV converts light into electric current using the photoelectric effect.

2.3.3 Wind Power

Wind Energy

- A large amount of energy is contained in wind. Since historical times man has used wind energy to drive pumps and mills. Windmills is a common feature of the landscape of Holland and Denmark.
- Wind energy depends largely on its speed, direction of the wind and the length of the period during which wind blows. Wind energy can be harnessed only when the average velocity of the wind is more than 32 km per hour. The ideal locations for the development of wind energy are coastal regions and wide open plains, where the velocity of wind is high.
- Wind power may be converted into electricity. Today research is going on to use wind to create a vacuum in a kind of silo which is able to take in air to power the turbine. If this research proves successful, wind energy will, make an important contribution in the energy budget of the near future.
- Wind energy has been developed on a large scale in most of the North-West and West European countries like France, U.K., Denmark, Netherlands, Norway, Sweden and Finland. In North America it is developed in- New England state and the Central plains.
- Rapid Progress has been made in the development of wind energy in India. Till 1996, a capacity of about 730 MW of wind power generation has been established. It was expected to reach 1000 MW by 1997. India would be the second exploiter of wind energy in the world, after U.S.A. The areas ideal for this energy are western coastal areas as well as Rajasthan.
- Wind power or wind energy is the use of wind to get mechanical power through wind turbines to turn electric generators and traditionally to do other work, such as milling or pumping.
- Wind farms have many wind turbines, which are connected to the transmission network. Onshore wind is an inexpensive source of electric power, cheaper than coal or gas plants.
- Power-management methods such as having dispatchable power sources, enough hydroelectric power, excess capacity, geographically distributed turbines, exporting and importing power to neighbouring areas, energy storage, or reducing demand when wind production is low, can in many cases overcome problems.
- In 2018, global wind power capacity grew 9.6% to 591 GW. In 2017, yearly wind energy production grew 17%, reaching 4.4% of worldwide electric power usage, and providing 11.6% of the electricity in the European Union.

- Wind power has been used as long as humans have put sails into the wind. Wind-powered machines used to grind grain and pump water, the windmill etc.
- The first windmill used for the production of electric power was built in Scotland in July 1887 by Prof James Blyth of Anderson's College.
- Nowadays, wind powered generators operate of every size range between tiny stations for battery charging at isolated residences, up to near-gigawatt sized offshore wind farms that provide electric power to national electrical networks.

Wind energy :

- Wind energy is the kinetic energy of air in motion, also called wind.
- Power is energy per unit time, so the wind power incident on A (e.g. equal to the rotor area of a wind turbine) is :
- Wind is the movement of air across the surface of the Earth, affected by areas of high pressure and of low pressure.
- The total amount of economically extractable power available from the wind is considerably more than present human power use from all sources.

Wind farms :

Table : 2.3 Large onshore wind farms

Wind farm	Capacity (MW)	Country
Gansu Wind Farm	7,965	China
Muppandal wind farm	1,500	India
Alta (Oak Creek-Mojave)	1,320	United States
Jaisalmer Wind Park	1,064	India
Shepherds Flat Wind Farm	845	United States
Roscoe Wind Farm	782	United States
Horse Hollow Wind Energy Center	736	United States
Capricorn Ridge Wind Farm	662	United States
Fântânele-Cogealac Wind Farm	600	Romania
Fowler Ridge Wind Farm	600	United States
Whitelee Wind Farm	539	United Kingdom

- A wind farm is a group of wind turbines in the same location used for production of electric power. A large wind farm may consist of several hundred individual wind turbines distributed over an extended area, but the land between the turbines may be used for agricultural or other purposes.

Offshore wind power :

- Offshore wind power refers to the construction of wind farms in water to generate electric power. These installations can utilize the more frequent and powerful winds that are available in these locations and have less impact on the landscape than land based projects. However, the construction and the maintenance costs are considerably higher.

- In 2010, 3.16 GW of offshore wind power capacity was operational, mainly in Northern Europe. Offshore wind power capacity is expected to reach a total of 75 GW worldwide by 2020, with significant contributions from China and the US.
- In a wind farm, individual turbines are interconnected with a medium voltage power collection system and communications network. At a substation, this medium-voltage electric current is increased in voltage with a transformer for connection to the high voltage electric power transmission system.

Mean wind speed in India :

- Wind power generation capacity in India has significantly increased in recent decades. As of 31 March 2019 the total installed wind power capacity was 36.625 GW, and it is the fourth largest installed wind power capacity in the world.
- Wind power costs in India are decreasing rapidly. The levelised tariff of wind power reached a record low of •2.43 (3.5¢ US) per kWh.

Installed capacity :

- The table below shows the India's year on year installed wind power capacity since 2005 :

Table 2.4 :Installed Wind Power Capacity

Fiscal	Year End Cumulative Capacity (in MW)
2005	6,270
2006	7,850
2007	9,587
2008	10,925
2009	13,064
2010	16,084
2011	18,421
2012	20,149
2013	21,264
2014	23,354
2015	26,769
2016	32,280
2017	34,046
2018	36,625

- Development of wind power in India began in 1952, when Thacker, a power engineer, initiated a project with the Indian Council of Scientific and Industrial Research (CSIR) to explore the possibilities of harnessing wind power in the country.
- The CSIR established a Wind Power Sub-Committee under P. Nilakantan and began detailed surveys of potential sites for harnessing the optimum amount of wind energy; it also successfully developed and tested large wood-and-bamboo windmills.

- In September 1954, E. W. Golding, a British power engineer and authority on wind energy generation, recommended extensive wind velocity surveys in different regions of India.
- Golding's recommendations were adopted by the CSIR in 1957. Regions of Saurashtra and Coimbatore had been identified as promising sites for generating electricity from wind power, and the Wind Power Sub-Committee had begun to contract 20 wind velocity survey stations across India, in addition to testing its indigenously designed windmills and obtaining a 6 kw.
- In 1960, the CSIR established a Wind Power Division as part of the new National Aeronautical Laboratory (NAL) in Bangalore, which was founded that year. From the 1960s into the 1980s, the NAL and other groups continued to carry out wind velocity surveys and develop improved estimates of India's wind energy capacity.
- Large-scale development of wind power began in 1985 with the first wind project in Veraval, Gujarat, in the form of a 40-kW Dutch machine connected to the grid.
- This machine was quite poor, it established the technical viability of operating wind turbines in the grid-connected mode in India.
- In 2015, the MNRE set the target for Wind Power generation capacity by the year 2022 at 60,000 MW.
- No offshore wind farm is under implementation as of December 2017. However, an Offshore Wind Policy was announced in 2015 and presently weather stations and LIDARs are being set up by NIWE at some locations.
- The first offshore wind farm is planned near Dhanushkodi in Tamil Nadu.

Electricity generation :
- Wind power accounts for nearly 10% of India's total installed power generation capacity and generated 62.03 TWh in the fiscal year 2018-19, which is nearly 4% of total electricity generation.

Table : 2.5 Monthly Electricity Generation in India April, 2018 - March, 2019

Month	North	West	South	East	North East	Total (GWh)
April 2018	552.54	1,604.27	1,165.93	-	-	3,322.74
May 2018	587.60	2,481.92	1,371.58	-	-	4,441.09
June 2018	1,035.61	3,461.16	3,827.89	12.28	-	8,336.94
July 2018	950.36	4,011.23	6,403.68	-	-	11,365.27
August 2018	910.12	3,730.76	7,129.62	1.15	-	11,771.66
September 2018	600.53	1,778.12	3,708.99	5.70	-	6,093.34
October 2018	209.39	744.69	1,864.79	3.91	-	2,789.24

Month	North	West	South	East	North East	Total (GWh)
November 2018	184.31	760.81	1,232.00	3.91	-	2,181.03
December 2018	283.01	1,333.62	1,163.33	9.29	-	2,789.24
January 2019	312.56	1,233.13	1,296.29	9.91	-	2,851.89
February 2019	385.01	1,313.14	1,384.07	12.25	-	3,094.47
March 2019	392.77	1,477.50	1,083.57	12.10	-	2,965.93
Total (GWh)	**6,403.79**	**23,930.36**	**31,631.72**	**70.50**	**-**	**62,036.38**

Wind power by state :

There is an increasing number of wind energy installations in states in India.

Table 2.6 : Installed wind capacity by state as of 31 March 2018

State	Total Capacity (MW)
Tamil Nadu	8,197
Gujarat	5,613
Maharashtra	4,784
Karnataka	4,509
Rajasthan	4,298
Andhra Pradesh	3,963
Madhya Pradesh	2,520
Telangana	101
Kerala	53
Others	4
Total	**34,043**

- Tamil Nadu's wind power capacity is around 29% of India's total.
- Maharashtra is one of the prominent states that installed wind power projects second to Tamil Nadu in India. As of end of March 2016, installed wind power capacity is 4655.25 MW.
- According to official data, wind power generations capacity in the state has increased a staggering ten times in last six years. Gujrat have 16% of total capacity of country.
- 4298 MW wind power plant has been installed in Rajasthan.
- Govt. of Madhya Pradesh has sanctioned another 15 MW project to Madhya Pradesh Windfarms Ltd. MPWL, Bhopal at Nagda Hills near Dewas under consultation from Consolidated Energy Consultants Ltd. CECL Bhopal.
- 55 MW production of wind power is installed in Kerala.
- The agency has identified 16 sites for setting up wind farms through private developers.
- Odisha a coastal state has higher potential for wind energy. Current installation capacity stands at 2.0 MW. Odisha has a windpower potential of 1700MW.

- The total installation in West Bengal is 2.10 MW till Dec 2009 at Fraserganj, South 24 Paraganas.
- The Kargil, Ladakh regions of Jammu and Kashmir state are potential wind energy areas, which are yet to be exploited.

Projects :
- India's largest wind power production facilities (10MW and greater)

Offshore wind power plants :
- India started planning in 2010 about offshore wind power.
- The project focuses on the States of Gujarat and Tamil Nadu for identification of potential zones for development through assessment.
- In September 2015, the India's cabinet has approved the National Offshore Wind Energy Policy. With this, the Ministry of New & Renewable Energy (MNRE) has been authorized as the Nodal Ministry for use of offshore areas within the Exclusive Economic Zone (EEZ)

2.3.4 Tidal Power

Wave Energy
- Waves like wind have energy to generate electricity. Tidal power has been successfully developed on the Rance Estuary in Brittany, France. But in the world there are probably only seven or eight sights where tidal energy can be harnessed. The initial development costs are also high.
- Wave energy can be utillsed, by' floating plants which can use the constant motion of the waves to drive turbines. But some areas are prone to storms which may destroy the power plants.
- Today this energy is harnessed only in the U.K., Russian Federation and Australia. The possibilities of erecting tidal power station in the Gulf of Cambay near Bhavnagar port of Gujarat and in the Sundarbans in West Bengal need serious examination.

Meaning :
- Tidal power or tidal energy is the form of hydropower that converts the energy obtained from tides into useful forms of power, mainly electricity.
- Although tidal energy has potential for future electricity generation. Tides are more predictable than the wind and the sun.
- Tidal energy has suffered from high cost and limited availability of sites with sufficiently high tidal ranges or flow velocities, thus restricting its total availability.
- The world's first large-scale tidal power plant was the Rance Tidal Power Station in France, which became operational in 1966.
- Tidal power is due to Earth's oceanic tides. Tidal forces are because of periodic variations in gravitational attraction of celestial bodies. These forces create corresponding motions or currents in the world's oceans.
- The magnitude and character of this motion reflects the changing positions of the moon and sun in relation to the earth, the effects of earth's rotation, and local geography of the sea floor and coastlines.

- Other natural energies exploited by humans originate directly or indirectly with the Sun, including fossil fuel, conventional hydroelectric, wind, biofuel, wave and solar energy.
- A tidal generator converts the energy of tidal flows into electricity.
- Because the Earth's tides are due to gravitational interaction with the Moon and Sun and the Earth's rotation, tidal power is inexhaustible and classified as a renewable energy resource.

Methods :

- Tidal power can be generated though four generating methods, which are as follows :

(i) Tidal stream generator :

- Tidal stream generators uses kinetic energy of moving water to power turbines, some tidal generators can be built into the structures of existing bridges or are entirely submersed.
- These turbines can be horizontal, vertical, open, or ducted types.
- Stream energy can be used at a much higher rate than wind turbines due to water being more dense than air.

(ii) Tidal barrage :

- Tidal barrages make use of the potential energy in the difference in height (or hydraulic head) between high and low tides.
- When using tidal barrages to generate power, the potential energy from a tide is seized through strategic placement of specialized dams.

(iii) Dynamic tidal power :

- Dynamic tidal power is an untried but promising technology that would exploit an interaction between potential and kinetic energies in tidal flows.

(iv) Tidal lagoon :

- A new tidal energy design option is to construct circular retaining walls embedded with turbines that can capture the potential energy of tides.
- The created reservoirs are similar to those of tidal barrages, except that the location is artificial and does not contain a pre-existing ecosystem.
- Tidal Energy, (Tidal Power) is classified as an alternate renewable energy. It is one of the forms of hydropower energy that exercises energy of the oceanic tides to generate electricity.
- Tide is the periodic shift or movement of vast quantities of water resulting from the gravitational forces of the sun and the moon acting on earth's water bodies. These vertical shifts or movement of water is known as tides.
- Normally each day experiences two high tides and two low tides. High tide is a situation where the water of the ocean bulges towards the shore.
- When the gravitational force between the Earth and the Moon is at right angles to each other, this gravitational force is weak and water flows in some other location.

Advantages of Tidal Energy Generation

(i) It has the potential to produce a great deal of free and green energy, thus, it is bio-friendly.

(ii) Tidal energy a renewable source of energy and its production has lower cost and its clean because it uses no fuel so it is environment-friendly and no waste by-products are produced either.

(iii) It is not expensive and is easy to maintain compared to other forms of renewable energy sources.

(iv) Low visual impact as the tidal turbines is mainly submerged beneath the water.

(v) Low noise pollution as any sound generated is transmitted through the water.

(vi) High predictability as high and low tides can be predicted years in advance and there is a definite surety of high and low tides occurring twice a day respectively.

(vii) Tidal barrages provide protection against flooding and land damage and tidal stream generators cause lesser or no harm to the natural landscape.

(viii) Large tidal reservoirs have multiple uses and can create recreational lakes and area.

Disadvantages of Tidal Energy Generation

(i) It requires a suitable site, where the tides and tidal streams are consistently strong and can be harnessed.

(ii) Tidal energy is not always a constant energy source because the energy generated from the tides depends completely on the strength and flow of the motions of the water, which itself is dependent on the gravitational effects of the celestial bodies- Earth, Moon, and the sun.

(iii) In addition to its installation and generation costs it should be able to withstand forces of nature thereby resulting in additional investment, apt construction and maintenance costs.

(iv) Only generates power ten hours a day during the outgoing and incoming of the tides.

(v) Chances of increase in coastal erosion where the tides are concentrated.

(vi) If not used properly it can create a mess in the form of accumulated silt, sediments and pollutants within the tidal barrage from rivers and streams flowing into the basin as it is unable to flow out into the sea.

(vii) Danger to marine animals like fish and other sea-life as they might get stuck in the barrage or get sucked by the force of tidal turbine blades.

(viii) Many types of advanced tidal energy generation techniques like dynamic tidal power and tidal lagoon still cannot be put in action because of the complexities attached to tidal energy generation.

Tidal Energy in India

- As of March 2017, India announced 7500 Km long coastline, where the height of high tide was recorded over 5 mtrs higher than the low tide which can essentially capture the potential tidal power.

- The Ministry of New and Renewable Energy estimated that the country can produce 7000 MW of power in the Gulf of Khambhat in Gujarat, 1200 MW of power in the Gulf of Kutch in Gujarat and about 100 MW of power in the Gangetic delta of Sunderbans in West Bengal.

- India ranks 81 positions in overall energy self-sufficiency at 66% in 2014.
- The primary energy consumption in India grew by 7.9% in 2018 and is the third biggest after China and USA with 5.8% global share.
- In 2017-18, the per-capita energy consumption is 23.355 Giga Joules (0.558 Mtoe) excluding traditional biomass use and the energy intensity of the Indian economy is 0.2332 Mega Joules per INR (56 kcal/INR).
- During the year 2018, the total investment in energy sector by India was 4.1% (US\$ 75 billion) of US\$ 1.85 trillion global investment.
- Indian solar power PV tariff has fallen to 2.44 (3.5¢ US) per kWh in May 2017 which is lower than any other type of power generation in India.

2.3.5 Geothermal Energy

Geothermal Energy :
- Some of the rain water percolates down through fractures in rock until it reaches the depth where it is heated by the magma. Once hot, the water rises from natural convection. Depending on temperature and pressure, the water can be turned to pure or dry steam or become a wet mixture of steam and water. It can be brought to the surface only through a natural fracture in the overlying rock or through a drilled well similar to that for oil and natural gas. When a successful well is drilled, it can supply steam for a thermal electrical plants operate on cost-free fuel once the well is found and successfully drilled.
- However, there are several problems in case of geothermal power.
(i) The resource of geothermal energy is very limited. Hence, its total world capacity to remain small.
(ii) The steam and water often contain salts and minerals that corrode and pit . Hence, further development in corrosion resistant metals is needed.
- The sites with largest potential generating capacities are located in central America, Italy, New Zealand, Philippines, Western U.S.A. and Iceland. The total world capacity is likely to remain small. There is at present about 69 GWe energy installed capacity worldwide.

Policy framework :
- India's strategy is the encouragement of the development of renewable sources of energy by the use of incentives by government including the use of nuclear energy (India Nuclear Cooperation Promotion Act), promoting windfarms and solar energy.
- A long-term energy policy perspective is provided by the Integrated Energy Policy Report 2006 which provides policy guidance on energy-sector growth.
- Recent fall in international oil prices due to shale oil production boom, would tilt the energy policy in favour of crude oil / natural gas.
- The energy policy wants to achieve self sufficiency, least pollution and long term sustainability.

Table 2.7

Purpose	Preferred fuel	Next preferred fuel	Least preferred fuel
Mobile military hardware	Indigenous diesel, Indigenous petrol	Ethanol, Biodiesel	Nil
Air transport	LNG	Biodiesel, Ethanol	ATF, HSK
Marine transport	LNG, FCEV, CNG	Pyrolysis oil, Nuclear fuel, Biodiesel, Ethanol	LDO, HFO, Bunker fuel, Diesel
Heavy duty road vehicles	LNG, FCEV, CNG, LPG	Biodiesel	Diesel, Animal draught power
Passenger four wheel vehicles	LPG, LNG, Battery power, FCEV	Biodiesel	Diesel, Petrol
Passenger two/three wheel vehicles	LPG, CNG, Battery power	Biodiesel	Petrol, Animal draught power
Railways	Electricity, LNG, LPG, FCEV	Biodiesel	Diesel
Illumination/ lighting	Electricity	CNG, LPG	Kerosene
Cooking	Electricity	CNG, Biochar	Kerosene, LPG, Fire wood
Space & water heating	Electricity, Pyrolysis oil, Biochar, Solar energy	CNG	Kerosene, LPG, Fire wood
Commercial / Domestic - appliances	Electricity	Battery power	Diesel, Petrol, LPG, CNG
Industrial- motive power	Electricity	Bio diesel, Pyrolysis oil	CNG, LPG, Diesel, Petrol
Industrial- heating	Biomass, Pyrolysis oil, Biochar, Solar thermal energy, Electricity	Biogas, PNG	Kerosene, LPG, Fire wood
Urea fertilizer	Biogas / synthetic gas, Biochar,	Natural gas, Electricity, Indigenous petcock	Naphtha, Coal
Water pumping	Electricity	LPG	Kerosene, Diesel, Petrol
Agriculture- heating & drying	Biomass, Pyrolysis oil, Solar energy	LPG, Electricity	Diesel, Petrol
Agriculture- appliances	Electricity, LPG	Bio diesel, Pyrolysis oil	CNG, Diesel, Petrol
Electricity Generation	Solar Power, Wind, Hydro power, biomass, Torrif acted biomass, Biochar, Biogas plant residue	CNG, Animal draught power (peaking power only), pumped-storage hydroelectricity (peaking power only)	Petrol, Diesel, NGL, LPG, LDO, HFO, Naptha, Nuclear, Coal, Petcoke

Purpose	Preferred fuel	Next preferred fuel	Least preferred fuel
Steel production	Renewable electricity, Charcoal, Biochar	Renewable hydrogen, LPG, CNG	Coke, Coal
Cement production	Indigenous petcock, Biomass, Waste organic matter, Renewable electricity	LPG, CNG	Coal
Protein rich cattle/fish feed	CNG, PNG, Biogas, LNG	SNG from coal, Coalbed methane, Coal mine methane, SNG from renewable electricity, SNG from indigenous petcock	Nil
Industrial- raw materials	As economically required	Nil	Nil

2.4 COMMERCIAL USAGE AND ROLE OF NATURAL RESOURCES IN THE DEVELOPMENT OF COMMERCE

Forests and Commerce

Forests play an important role in commerce. Various commercial activities are related to forests. They can be summarised as follows :

(1) Forest based industries

These industries are dependent for their raw materials which are obtained from the forests. Main among them are :

(a) Primary forest industries :

These are saw milling, plaining of wood, manufacturing pulp and paper, plywood and penal products, wood-seasoning and preservation, tanning, etc. In Russian Federation, Canada the U.S.A., Norway, Sweden, Finland, Germany, large areas are covered by coniferous forests. In these countries, these primary forest industries play an important role in commerce. They are the major producers of saw wood, pulp and paper. A large number of people are engaged in forest industries.

(b) Secondary forest industries :

• These industries process the forest products and bring the output of forests closer to human consumption. These industries manufacture sports and athletic goods, matches, crates, drums, barrels, furniture and cabinets, bullock cart and agricultural tools and implements, body of trucks and railway coaches, structural wooden goods, posts, doors and windows, artificial. limbs, boats, toys, pencils, musical instruments, packing cases, photo-frames, rifles, shuttles, blocks, handles, drawing and mathematical instruments, wood carving, wooden utensils, and host of others. Besides providing a wide range of products, these industries also provide employment to a large number of people.

(2) Activity of construction :

* Forests give an adequate supply coxo fictional of materials. Although there are many substitutes for wood, we shall always) require large quantities of wood for our purpose. Especially in the temperate lands of the world, where winters are long and very cold, use wood for making houses as they remain warm in winter. Thus the activity of construction depends largely on forests.

(3) Lumbering :

* Though lumbering is practiced on a small scale in many of the forests. it provides continuous and stabilised employment in the coniferous forests of the world. In the continuous forests of Canada, the U.S.A., Norway, Sweden, Denmark, Russian Federation lumbering is practiced throughout the year and a large number of people are engaged in lumbering.

(4) Gathering of forest products :

* In the equatorial and monsoon forests of the world, collection of forest products is a major activity. Here various useful parts of the trees are collected on a commercial basis by the native people and are then used for various purposes or are exported, e.g. chickle found in the equatorial forests is used for making popular chewing gum; balata is used for making undersea cables and golf ball covers: the leaves of the tendu trees in Madhya Pradesh in India are used for making bidis. Thus, these activities have an important role to uplift the rural people by providing them job opportunities.

(5) Trade :

* Forests occupy important place in national as well as international trade. As today distribution of forests is very uneven, the geographic separation of forest product demand and supply regions makes international trade an important factor in the forest industry. Most of the trade occurs among highly developed countries as they can afford to buy the products. Japan, South Korea and several West European countries import nearly 82 percent of unmilled wood. Malaysia is the leading exporter of this wood. Shaped wood exports are dominated by Canada & Sweden, the U.S.A., Finland and Austria. Pulpwood is the most important commodity that enters in the world trade. Canada, the U. S. A. and Scandinavian countries (Norway, Sweden and Finland) are the major exporters while Germany, Japan, Italy, France and the U.K. are the major importers.
* Besides these commodities, a very large variety of wooden articles is sold in national markets. Forests also provide raw materials for Cottage and Small Scale Industries and many products like articles made of carved sandlewood are sold all over the world.

(6) Direct employment :

* Direct employment is provided by the forest service in the form of management technical, research, planning and executive jobs. Recruitments for these various jobs are made through various competitive exams held in urban areas.

(7) Tourism :

- The forests are also important for tourism as they have a recreational function. They add the scenic beauty to the landscape. The temperate deciduous forests are particularly noted for their beauty as before the fall season, the leaves of different colours add unfathomable charm to the landscape. The forests are also the homes of wild life. Thus the national parks of various .countries invite tourists from all over the world. Tourism is not only an industry, it is also an invisible trade. The foreign tourists are very important as they bring with them the valuable foreign currency.

(8) Transport and other economic activities :

- Through transport the forest products are carried from areas of production to the areas of consumption. Increased means of transport, especially water transport is necessary as the majority of the forest products are bulky and heavy. Forests also provide employment facilities in the field of transport.
- Forestry, the trade and transport of forest products also create employment opportunities in the growing field of banking, insurance, warehousing, advertising and publicity.
- Thus forests play an important role in commerce.

2.4.1 Natural Resources in the Process of Development

- The economic development of a country affected significantly by the presence or absence of favorable natural resources. In fact, most developed countries make the best use of the natural resources available to them.
- Any underdeveloped country beginning its journey of economic development has to start with and concentrate on the development of available natural resources.
- They help in increasing the level of living and purchasing power. An increased purchasing power helps get foreign exchange which is then used to purchase capital equipment. This sets the development process in motion.
- Natural resources include land, water sources, fisheries, mineral resources, marine resources, forests, rainfall, climate, and topography, and there are many unknown resources too.
- As a country increases its knowledge about the unknown resources and their use, its natural endowment is materially altered.
- India has a total geographical area of around 329 million hectares. However, we have statistical information of only around 306 million hectares.
- Forests have been the most important natural resources because of timber, wood for fuel, and fodder to a wide range of non-wood products, forests play a critical role in environmental and economic sustainability.
- Around the world, India is one of the wettest countries, and receives an average annual rainfall of around 1100 mm.
- 2 million square kilometers of Exclusive Economic Zone for deep-sea fishing
- 7,520 kilometers of coastline
- 29,000 kilometers of rivers

- 1.7 million hectares of reservoirs
- Around 1 million hectares of brackish water area
- 0.8 million hectares of tanks and ponds for inland as well as marine fish production
- India have still has not exploited these resources completely.
- The industrial growth of a nation depends largely on the development and management of its mineral resources. For example, coal and iron are required for the growth and development of the iron and steel industry.
- Mineral fuels like petroleum, coal, thorium and uranium are of national importance.
- Today, we have degraded our physical environment and rapid economic progress is turning our country into a vast wasteland. Here are some areas, where India is witnessing extreme levels of environmental degradation due to economic development:
- Overgrazing led to ecological degradation.
- Deforestation led to land degradation as well as soil erosion.
- Irresponsible and faulty utilization of water resources has caused adverse environmental effects.
- Industrialization has also led to atmospheric pollution.
- Mining has led to certain environmental problems.

Points to Remember

- Natural Resources exist on earth without the indulgence of humans.
- Sources of Natural Resources :
  - (i) According to source of Origin :
    - (a) Biotic
    - (b) Abiotic
  - (ii) According to stage of development :
    - (a) Potential Resources
    - (b) Actual Resources
    - (c) Reserve resources
    - (d) Stock Resources
  - (iii) According to Renewability :
    - (a) Renewable Resources
    - (b) Non-Renewable Resources
  - (iv) According to aims and purpose :
    - (a) Natural Resources
    - (b) Human Resources
  - (v) Renner's Classification
    - (a) Inexhaustible Resources
    - (b) Exhaustible Resources
  - (vi) On the basis of Distribution :
    - (a) Localised
    - (b) Ubiquitous
  - (vii) According to natural of ownership :
    - (a) Individual Resources
    - (b) National Resources
    - (c) International Resources

- Classification of Forests :
  (a) Tropical :
  (1) Evergreen of Equatorial forests   (2) Deciduous or Monsoon Forests
  (b) Temperate :
  (1) Deciduous   (2) Evergreen and coniferous
- Non-conventional Energy :
  Resources : (a) Solar Energy   (b) Wind energy
  (c) Wave/Tidal energy   (d) Geothermal Energy

Questions for Discussion

Q. (I) Answer the following questions :

1. What is the meaning of Resources ?
2. What is the nature of Natural Resources ?
3. Give the classification of Resources ?
4. What are the uses of Resources ?
5. What is the importance of Natural Resources ?
6. What is the role of the Forests in Commerce ?
7. What are the types of Forests ? What are their characteristics ?
8. What is the Societal Significance of Forests ?
9. What is the importance of Forests ?
10. What do you understand by Non-conventional Resources ? What are the types of Non-conventional Resources ?
11. What is Solar Energy ? What are the limitations ?
12. Write in detail about Solar energy in India.
13. What is Thermal Energy ? What are it's applications ?
14. What do you understand by Wind Power ? What is offshore wind power ?
15. Write in detail about the Wind Power generation in India ?
16. What is Tidal power ? What are the methods of Tidal power generation ?
17. What is India's strategy in developing renewable sources of energy ?
18. How Natural Resources help in the process of development ?

Q. (II) Short Notes :

1. Natural Resources
2. Evergreen or Equatorial forests
3. Characteristics of Monsoon forests
4. Forests
5. Solar Energy
6. Wind Energy
7. Tidal Energy
8. Thermal Energy

Chapter **3**...

Role of Industries and Geographical Significance (Indian Context)

Contents ...

Learning Objectives ...

➢ To Comprehend the importance of geographic location and its commercial usage.

➢ To Study manufacturing Industries and handicrafts in the world as commercial activities.

➢ To acquaint the students with the importance of localization process and sourcing Industries from commercial point of view.

INTRODUCTION

Manufacturing is a secondary economic activity of man. It depends on the products available in nature. The products obtained from nature are made into more useful forms. Modern manufacturing started with the invention of the steam engine and machines and the use of coal as a source of power. The Industrial Revolution began in Europe and then spread to different parts of the world. However, industries are not equally developed in all countries. Industrialisation is a barometer to measure the economic progress of a country. Those countries which have a large number of industries with a large amount of invested capital, a large industrial labour force and large industrial output are considered to be developed countries of the world, e.g. the U. S.A. and Japan are the highly industrialised developed countries. On the other hand, the developing countries of the world are those which present an opposite picture in the field of industries.

3.1 ROLE OF INDUSTRIES IN THE ECONOMIC DEVELOPMENT AND FACTORS AFFECTING INDUSTRIAL LOCATION, BUSINESS LOCATIONS AND IT'S GEOGRAPHICAL IMPLICATIONS

3.1.1 Industrial Economics (Meaning)

There is no consensus on the name of the subject, some title it as 'Economics of Industry', 'Industry and Trade', 'Industrial Economics', or title it as 'Industrial Organisation'. There are two broad elements of industrial economics. The first one known as the descriptive element is concerned with the information content of the subject. It aims at providing the businessman with a survey of the industrial organisations of his own country and of other countries with which he might come in contact. It would give him full information regarding the natural resources, industrial climate in the country, supplies of factors of production etc. The second element of the subject is concerned with the business policy and decision-making. This is analytical part dealing with topics such as market analysis, pricing, choice of techniques, location of plant, labour etc. The two elements are interdependent and not competitive.

Definitions :

(i) **J. L. Hanson** defines Industrial Economics as, *"A term for economic analysis as applied to industry". This branch of applied economics assumed greater importance with the development of business schools."*

(ii) **Penguin** (Dictionary of Economics) states *"Industrial Economics is a general term for that branch of applied economics which deals with the factors affecting the structure of industry and the way it is owned and managed. It can be thus, regarded as an area of applied micro-economics."*

(iii) **Harper Collins :** *"Industrial Economics is the branch of economics concerned with the functioning of the price system. Industrial economics examines the relationship between market structure and market performance using the analytical framework of the theory of markets within an empirical and dynamic setting."*

Scope of Industrial Economics :

- The scope of industrial economics is very vast. It embraces analytical and descriptive economic analysis as a branch of applied economics.
- Following are the areas or fields of its study that indicate the scope of Industrial Economics :

(i) Introduction to Industrialisation : Industrial Economics consists of meaning and scope of industrial economics, concepts of firm and industry, rationale of industrial policy, Policy Resolution 1948, 1951, 1956, 1990, 1991 critical appraisal, licensing and fiscal policies, industrial MRTP, FERA structures, changes and choices in Indian Industry.

(ii) Size and Location : The subject includes economies of size, theories, optimum size, reconciliation of optima, factors affecting size, industrial location, factors affecting location, government intervention, industrial dispersal policy and industrial estates.

(iii) Industrial Combinations : It includes the diversification of industries, industrial combinations, monopolies, survival of small firms, mergers, Government policy, multinationals, foreign collaborations etc.

(iv) Concentration of Economic Power : Industrial economics contains monopoly, concentration of economic power, state policy and Mahalanobis Committee.

(v) Industrial Productivity : Industrial Economics includes productivity norms, methods of measuring productivity; productivity and production, factors affecting industrial efficiency; profitability, its measurement, Productivity in Indian Industry; national Productivity Council etc.

(vi) Growth of Modern Industry : It includes review of industrial growth during the plan period, policy changes, dispersal of industry, balanced regional development in India, pattern and growth of industries in public and co-operative sector in India.

(vii) Structure of Industries in India : Study of structure and problems of industries in India with reference to location, size, production trends, productivity, exports regarding cotton textiles, cement, sugar, coal, iron and steel etc.

(viii) Industrial Relations : This part of industrial economics contains study on industrial disputes, role of government, code of discipline, collective bargaining, joint consultation, wage boards etc. It also contains objectives, growth rate of trade unions, weakness, evaluation of trade unions etc.

(ix) Progress of Industries : It explains industrial progress under planned economy, priorities for industrial development, progress under First, Second, Fourth upto Ninth Five Year Plan.

(x) Labour Welfare : It handles state and labour welfare, welfare schemes, estimates etc.

(xi) Workers Participation on Management : It deals with the forms, benefits, labour conference, study groups etc.

(xii) Industrial Sickness : It studies causes, consequences of industrial sickness. Measures to remedy sickness in industries.

(xiii) Rationalisation : Industrial economics includes aspects of rationalisation, importance of rationalisation, attitude of employees towards rationalisation and opposition by labour.

3.1.2 Objectives of Industrial Economics

Objectives : The objectives of Industrial Economics are as follows :

(a) The Broad Objectives of Industrial Economics and Traditional Micro-Economics :

- The broad objective of industrial economics is the development of satisfactory explanations of the ways in which economic forces operate within the industrial sector. This is identical to the broad objective of micro-economic theory.

(b) Particular Objectives in Industrial Economics and the Conflict between Realism and Generality : Whilst the two approaches (traditionally associated with industrial economics and micro-economic theory) may share the same broad objective, they may be pursuing different objectives at the particularised level. The degree of realism required in any economic analysis involves reference to the particular objective involved and the achievement of a suitable compromise between the desire to maintain reality and the desire to achieve the maximum generality in the findings. The ideal balance between the particular and the general in economic analysis will vary accordingly.

(c) Industrial Economics and Management Disciplines : The relationship between the objectives of industrial economics and those of business or managerial economics also requires classification. Managerial and Business Economics can be distinguished from Industrial Economic in two ways :

(i) Firm Aims to Maximise Profits : Most of the writings on managerial economics starts from the assumption that the firm aims to maximize its profits and then proceeds to examine the manner in which the decision rules and procedures of the firm should be formulated in order to achieve its stated objective.

- Above all, as a branch of social science, industrial economics will be interested in what actually happens as distinct from what should happen in hypothetical or ideal circumstances. While there is a difference in approach, these two types of study are related. The future development of managerial economics, therefore, partly depends upon further advances in Industrial Economics.

(ii) Interdisciplinary : Managerial Economics is interdisciplinary in a way and to a degree that does not apply to industrial economics, although other social science disciplines do have a contribution to make to the study of industrial economics. Because of multi-disciplinary nature of the subject it is most usefully studied after a preliminary study of the main disciplines, including industrial economics, upon which it draws.

Industrial Location :

(a) Ideal Location of Factory / Plant (Meaning) : In setting up a factory, a manufacturer has to take three inter-related decisions simultaneously.

- (i) The scale of operation.
- (ii) The technique to be adopted while selecting appropriate combination of factors of production.
- (iii) The location of the factory.

The conventional theory of the firm provides the rules or norms for the first two types of decisions to be taken. But it ignores the third one completely.

(b) Locational Decision Making : A separate branch of economics bordering with the discipline of geography, which is known as 'Industrial Location' or 'Locational Analysis' deals with the elements of the locational decision-making.

(c) Decision Making not Simple : The task of decision-making about industrial location is not very simple. A manufacturer has to consider several technical, economical and institutional factors. Location of industries means the methods and desirability of concentrating industries in different areas or localities. Further, each manufacturer has to find out from time to time whether favourable conditions still continue for the location of an industry.

Each industrialist will try to locate his unit at a place where the cost of production is lowest. This is called location of industries. On the other hand, when the industries are concentrated in a particular area, it is called localisation of industries which can be due to main reasons including physical location, availability of raw materials, labour etc. In short, locating a business involves a large relatively permanent investment. If the selection is improper, the manufacturer incurs a heavy loss. Thus, the site has to be carefully selected, that which may provide maximum advantage.

(d) Stages of Location : The problem of site selection of a factory can be solved in the following three stages :
(1) Selection of the region.
(2) Selection of the locality.
(3) Selection of actual site.

(1) Selection of the Region : Normally, the geographical area is divided on the basis of natural regions or political boundaries within the nation. For instance, Maharashtra State, Uttar Pradesh State etc. which region is suitable for location will be considered on the basis of comparative cost advantage.

(2) Selection of the Locality : Next to the selection of region, follows the selection of specific locality within the region. While selecting the locality following options are there –
(i)   Urban area.
(ii) Rural area.
(iii) Sub-urban area.
- The comparative advantages of each locality are considered at this stage.

(3) Selection of Actual Site : While making decisions on the selection of site certain facilities and factors have to be considered. For instance the type of development of land, cost of levelling, possibility of plant expansion, availability of infrastructural facilities like banking, power, communication, postal services etc.

Various Factors Affecting Industrial Location :
- **Factors Affecting Industrial Location :**

(I) Primary Factors :
- The primary factors considered while planning the industrial location are :

(a) Supply of Raw Materials :

- It is necessary to consider the adequate supply of raw materials and the nature of raw materials. The cost of raw materials is also an important element. Further there should be regular supply of raw material. The time and cost required for transporting the raw material is also to be considered. Considering all these factors industrial units are mostly located near the sources of raw material.

(b) Nearness to Market :

- In those industries where raw materials are obtained easily from different places, nearness to sources of raw material is not an important as nearness to the market. It is important for supplying goods to the customers in a minimum period of time adjusting supply according to changes in demand and gaining control over the market. It is an important factor in case of industries producing light, delicate and perishable goods e.g. cosmetics, food products, fashionable goods having a changing demand etc. Nearness to market helps the industries to take advantages of favourable prices and demand in the market.

(c) Transport Facilities :

- Speedy transport facilities are needed for the regular and timely supply of raw materials at low cost and for transporting finished products on time to the market. A producer has to chose a speedy and cheap means of transport after making a comparative cost study of different means of transport e.g. roads, railways, waterways, etc.

(d) Supply of Labour :

- Availability of labour and particularly of skilled labour and technicians have a great influence on the location of industries. In case of industries where not much of sophisticated skills are required, industries tend to move to areas with abundant supplies of cheap labour e.g. cotton textile industry. On the other hand, industries requiring skilled labour as in case of electronics industries, the tendency will be to move to relatively urban areas where such skilled laboures concentrate. Further, attraction of an industry towards labour centres will depend on the ratio of labour cost to the total cost of production.

(e) Power :

- All types of industries where big or small require power. With the advent of electricity, influence of coal as a location determining factor has lessened. So, today electricity is the main source of industrial energy. It can be transported from place to place. Therefore, along with the availability of electricity in adequate quantity. The rate of electricity is also considered. Places offering rate facilities attract industries in that location and mostly those requiring considerable amount of power.

(f) Supply of Capital :

- Industries require capital for initial promotion and expansion. Large scale industries require large amounts of equity capital and debenture capital for a long period. It is therefore necessary that development banks or financial institutions are developed. Capital is more mobile than labour and therefore nearness to capital is not very important for the purpose of location of industries.

(II) Secondary Factors :

The secondary factors which influence the industrial location are :

(a) Natural Factor :

- For industrial location, the study of land site is very important because in economics, land includes not only the surface of the soil but also water, minerals, forest wealth, rivers, coastline etc. This is important in case of some industries like cotton textiles, sugar and jute. In case of industries requiring minerals and which are heavy for the purpose of transport, industries using such material will locate in areas of their sources. Similarly, water and climate also affect the localization of industries.

(b) Historical and Religious Factors :

- Some industrial cities are of historical and religious importance. For example, the sarees of Banaras, the Kolhapuri chappals, the shawls of Kashmir etc. Due to these historical and religious importance industries are also located at such places.

(c) Entrepreneurship :

- Presence of entrepreneurship plays an important role in establishment of industry at any particular place. Some may prefer to live and work with people of their own community. Therefore, they may prefer to start industries in their home town or states. This is particularly in developing countries where entrepreneurship is an extremely scarce factor unequally distributed in different parts of the country and among different communities.

(d) Personal Factors :

- In the business history, personal consideration have also affected the location of certain industrial units. There is no rationale for such considerations, however, when there is a possibility of multiple location, this factor plays a decisive role in locational consideration. Henry Ford started the automobile industry in Detroit (U. S. A.) because it was his home town. In course of time, roads, ancillary industries came to be provided and growth of automobile industries attracted other industries to that place.

(e) Strategic Considerations :

- Location of basic industries is greatly influenced by strategic considerations. Safe location assumes great importance. For example, India has to consider the neighbouring countries while determining the location of defense and armament industries.

(f) External Economics :

- When a particular industry comes to be concentrated at a particular place, it influences the choice of location of various other industries as external economies are experienced due to specialized subsidiary activities. The external economies constitute an enterprising spirit, innovation, technical know - how and an industrious nature of population.

(g) Government Subsidies and Facilities :

- The government may encourage industries in underdeveloped areas by making capital, land, water, power etc. available at subsidised rates by way of development rebate, tax exemptions, price subsidies water and power at cheap rate, constructing roads and railway hires etc. By giving these facilities, the government may bring about the development of industries in backward areas and this will result in the regional balancing of industries.

(h) Miscellaneous Factors :

- The following miscellaneous factors also affect the location of industries.
    (i)   Disposal of wastes,
    (ii) Availability of recreational, medical and educational facilities,
    (iii) Community attitudes,
    (iv) Ecological and environmental considerations,
    (v)   Availability of facilities like schools, hospitals, post offices, parks etc.

'3.1.3 Role of Industries in Economic Development

Role of Industries in Economic Development :

- The, power and wealth of advanced countries are based on industrial wealth. The process of industrialisation is associated with the development of mechanical knowledge attitudes and skills of industrial work and is also equally beneficial to the growth of various related sectors of economy.

Let us study the role of industries in economic development of a country.

1.   Boost the Primary sector :

- The industries require constant flow of raw materials which is obtained from various sources like mines, forests, oceans, farms, grasslands, etc. If raw materials are not available in nearby areas, then they are also brought .from distant lands. Before the introduction of modern machinery, manufacturing was carried out on a small scale as the requirement of raw materials was very limited. But the modern Industries consume huge quantities of raw materials for their large scale production. Hence, this activity has boosted many primary activities of man through which the raw materials are obtained.

- Today forest based industries produce wood-pulp, paper, synthetic fibres on an unprecedented scale due to ever-increasing demand for these products. Hence lumbering is practiced on a commercial scale in the coniferous forests of the world. The economic development of Canada, Norway, Sweden, Finland and Russian Federation which have large areas under these forests is partly due to the large scale forestry. Industries require constant supplies of variety of minerals. Thus, today mining is practiced in many parts of the world on a commercial scale. The countries like South Africa, Middle East countries have their prosperous economies due to large scale mining. Oil has become a boon to Middle East Countries due to ever-increasing demand for oil and oil products form various industries.

- Industries started manufacturing agricultural machinery like tractors and combine harvestors which enabled the American farmers to bring the vast prairies under extensive mechanised grain farming. The introduction of pneumatic tyres was responsible for bringing large areas under rubber in plantation agriculture of S.E. Asian countries. The food-processing industries created large scale demand for milk to make milk-powder, cheese and butter; Meat packing industries wanted meat for packing, hence it became possible to bring large areas of Australia, New Zealand, Argentina under cattle rearing. Without these industries and their refrigeration facilities, these perishable products would not have reached the distant markets. Today fish processing industries use fish on a large scale thus encourage commercial fishing. The special ships made for undersea mining have made possible to collect minerals from the ocean floors.

- Thus, the primary activities are in many countries of the world are practiced on a scale largely due to industries to fulfill their demand of raw materials. The economies of many of the developing countries are becoming prosperous due to these commercial activities. The credit to bring prosperity to these countries goes directly to industries which consume the raw materials to convert them into more useful forms.

2. **Development of Transportation :**

- The automobile industries are responsible for manufacturing different modes of transportation like cars, railways, ships and aeroplanes which have revolutionalised the world. These industries introduced the automobiles which are able to carry passengers and goods on a large scale from one part of the world to the other. New world was discovered, people started settling in America and Australia. Minerals, forest products, agricultural produce are now sent from the areas of production to the distant markets also. Transportation arteries made it possible to set the industries even in those areas which lack the basic raw materials, e.g. Japan. We cannot imagine the prosperous economy of Japan without her ships which bring in raw materials from different parts of the world and export back the manufactured goods in the world market.

3. **Benefited Trade :**

- The manufacturing activity has also benefited the economic activity of trade. The industries create a large scale demand, for raw materials and at the same time they also want market for their manufactured goods. Thus, the trade of raw materials and manufactured goods has started not only at the national level but also at an international level. The prosperity of the Middle East countries is due to their export of oil; the economic development of Japan is due to large scale import of raw materials, manufacturing and export of manufactured goods. Manufacturing has also influenced the internal trade, e.g. jute goods made in West Bengal and bicycles made in Punjab are sold all over India.

4. **Improvement in the living standards :**

- Industrialisation improves living standards of the people. The industrial workers get cash income which is fixed. It is not flexible like farmers whose income fluctuates with famines and floods. As a result, industrial worker has more money to spend on consumer goods. These workers form a large market for consumer goods and in turn lead to greater industrial development.

- Industrialisation improves living standard of the people. The industrial workers get cash income which is fixed. It is not flexible like farmers whose income depends on famines and floods. As a result, industrial worker has more money to spend on consumer goods, on his children's education, etc. These workers purchase from a large market for manufactured goods and which in turn lead to greater industrial development.

- Thus, hundreds of millions of people depend on industries for food, shelter, cloth luxuries. Manufacturing is closely related to other occupations, For example 'them for raw materials for factories depends on. The positions of the chief nations as world powers of today depend to a large degree upon the extent to which they engage in modern manufacturing.

- Creating prosperous economies industries are also important for the following :

5. **Self-sufficiency :** A country can produce a large variety of goods instead -of relying on imports. This increasing self-sufficiency gives greater political and economic strength.

6. **Employment for excess population :** Most of the developing countries have rapidly growing populations. Industrialisation is seen as the best way of providing large number of jobs for the unemployed.

- Thus, hundreds of millions of people depend on industries for food, shelter, clothing, tools and a large number of items which make life comfortable. Manufacturing is closely related to other occupations, since it depends on them for raw materials for factories foodstuffs for workers and markets for manufactured articles. The positions of the chief nations as world power today and their economic development depends to a large degree upon the extent to which they engage in modern manufacturing.

Industries have an important role to play in the economic development of India

(1) Generates Employment :

- 70% of India's labour force is engaged in the Primary section i.e. agriculture. 'But Indian agriculture is unable to absorb a larger number of workers in a productive way. The Industrial sector can absorb greater number of workers.

- Industries not only provide employment but a higher income and will help to improve the living standard of the Indian people.

- However the effect of a low percentage of industrial labour is reflected per capita income.

(2) Economic Growth :

- Modernization and prosperity of agriculture is not the solution to India's economic progress. The demand for agricultural commodities like tea and coffee is highly elastic in the world market. The developed countries in the world have also developed agriculture and they have also introduced numerous synthetic substances like synthetic rubber and plastic to replace certain natural products.

- Thus, India can no longer depend upon foreign trade in agricultural commodities for its economic development. It has to depend on industrial growth.

(3) Agro-based Industries :

- India produces a vast range of industrial raw material like cotton, jute, oil-seeds, minerals and several others. Instead of exporting these valuable raw materials, India is able to set up a large number of agro-based industries like cotton-textiles, jute industries, sugar industries which can absorb a larger labour force which will earn a rising level of income. These agro-based industries will also create job opportunities in the quaternary and tertiary sectors of economic activities.

(4) Complementary Progress :

- The growth of agriculture and industries goes hand in hand. Agricultural progress brings prosperity to, the farmers. Due to a high income, the purchasing power of the farmers increases which' results in the increasing demand for industrial products. This accelerated demand boosts industrialisation.

(5) Higher per capita Income :

- Rapid industrialisation in India will not only create more demand for food-grains and industrial raw materials but more people will be displaced from the agricultural sector through the introduction of industrial goods like tractors and other such machines. These people will get jobs in the developing industries in India.

- Thus, more people will be absorbed in high productivity occupation. The net value of output per person is higher in industry than in agriculture. Thus, the. changing occupational structure of the people will be reflected in a higher per capita income. With the rise in income levels people want to spend more on manufactured goods- than on food.

- Thus, industries play an important role in the economy of the country and with a vast network of small-scale, medium and large-scale modern. industries, India will soon have a developed and prosperous economy.

(6) Exploitation of resources :

- Industries are capable of utilizing all the resources present in the economy. They can even make use of scraps and waste materials. Agriculture cannot make use of all the resources.

(7) Foreign exchange :

- India cannot earn adequate foreign exchange from the exports of its primary products. It is because of the fact that the demand for such products is very low in other countries. Industrial exports need to be added to the primary products.

(8) Balanced development :

- Indian economy is not a balanced economy. Our greater dependence on agriculture has made us poor. With the industrialization in the economy this anomaly can be removed. If agriculture is the backbone of the economy, industry is the energy.

(9) Self-sustained growth :

- The rapid progress in of capital goods industries promote the growth of agriculture, transport and communication. It also enables the country to produce a variety of consumer goods in large quantities and at low costs.
- It also eliminates our dependence on other countries for the supply of essential goods and makes us self-sufficient.

(10) Nation's security :

- Dependence on foreign countries for defense goods is always risky affair. We do not have good relations with our neighboring countries especially Pakistan and China.

3.1.4 Factors Affecting Industrial Location

- Industries are not equally developed in all parts of the world because their location depends on several factors. Industries are normally located in those favourable areas where is advantages are greater than the disadvantages. The following are the major factors that affect the location of industries.

(1) Raw Material :

- The raw materials used in manufacturing come mainly from farms, forests, fisheries, mines and quarries. Industries require a constant supply of raw materials. Thus the location of industries is largely influenced by the nature of the raw material.

(a) Heavy, bulky and cheap raw materials :

- Raw materials like timber and minerals are bulky, heavy and cheap. Further more, these raw materials lose their weight in the process of manufacturing. In such cases, the related industries develop near the sources of these raw materials in order to save the heavy transportation cost of these materials, e.g. plants manufacturing cement are found near the source of the raw materials used.

(b) Bulky and perishable raw materials :

- Raw materials that are perishable must be processed immediately near their source areas. Hence, food processing plants like dairy creamery, fruit canning, as well as sugar mills are located near the source of the raw materials. The dairy creameries are located in the dairy farming areas of Netherlands and New Zealand and the sugar factories are developed in the sugarcane growing areas U.P., Bihar and Maharashtra in India.

(c) Light, non-weight losing raw materials :
Raw material like ginned cotton is a non-perishable material that does not lose any weight in the manufacturing process. Such industries are set up mostly in the market areas.

(d) Manufactured raw materials :

- Sometimes, a manufactured final product of one industry is used as a raw material for another industry. In such cases, both these industries are found in one region, e.g. the heavy railways manufacturing plants use steel from iron and steel industries and are always located where iron and steel industries are set up.

(e) Imported raw materials :
- Many countries lack in one or the other raw material and these are imported from other countries, mainly by cheap water transport. Thus, the raw material arrives first at the ports. In order to reduce the cost of inland transportation, industries develop at the ports. That is why-a majority of ports in the world are important industrial centres e.g. London, Shanghai, Singapore and Mumbai.

(2) Power :
- Coal, oil and electricity are the major power resources which are indispensable in running manufacturing plants. These different power resources affect the location of industries in different ways :

(a) Coal : Coal is cheap and bulky. Heavy cost is involved in its transportation. Hence, industries that use coal as a power resource are always located near the coal-fields. All over the world, coal-fields are major industrial regions, e.g. Damodar Valley in India.

(b) Oil : Oil and 'gas can be easily transported through oil tankers, wagons and pipelines. Hence industries that use oil as a power resource are not especially located near the oil fields.

(c) Electricity : Electricity can be transmitted conveniently within a radius of 640 km. from its point of generation. Hence, industries relying on electricity are largely dispersed and are not necessarily, located near the source of supply. Industries located in Mumbai use electricity generated at the Bhivpuri, Khopoli and Koyna power stations.

(3) Transport :
- Manufacturing plants require a constant supply of raw materials and at the same time they have to send their manufactured goods to the markets. The raw materials are brought either from nearby areas or from distant countries. Similarly, manufactured goods are sent either to local, national or international markets. High transportation cost is involved if the sources of raw materials or the market lie far away from the manufacturing plants. Thus, low cost of transportation is the key factor in the location of manufacturing industries. The cost of transportation can be minimised in the following ways :

(a) If the raw material is bulky, heavy and is much more in weight as compared to its finished products, the industries are set up near the sources of such raw materials. e.g. smelting of minerals is usually carried out near the mining areas. Industries based on timber are located near forests.

(b) If the final product is easily breakable like chinaware and glassware, the transportation charges are high as these goods have to be insured and require careful handling. Factories producing such goods generally develop near the markets.

(c) If the raw material is brought from distant countries through waterways, the usually industries are usually located near the ports. Such location saves the cost of further inland transportation. Many of Japan's industries are based on imported raw materials.

These materials first arrive at the ports. Naturally the industries have developed at the port cities of Japan e.g. Nagasaki, Kawasaki and Kyoto.

(d) Railways provide an efficient and cheap means o transportation for carrying bulky commodities. Usually the railway junctions provide ideal locations for industries, e.g. Kanpur in India and Chicago in the U. S. A.

(e) Rivers and canals also provide very cheap means of transportation. Thus, numerous industries develop along these arteries. With the opening of the Great Lakes St. Lawrence Sea way of North America, a string of industries has developed along this route. West Bengal is a major producer of jute. Its jute mills have developed along the river Hooghly which transports the raw materials and as well as finished products cheaply.

(4) Market :

People create the demand for manufactured goods and thus form markets. Markets depend on two factors :

(a) Number of people : Densely populated areas create a large demand and form a wide market for goods.

(b) Purchasing power of people : People in developing countries have a low purchasing power. Thus, the densely populated areas of such countries do not create markets except for goods necessary for life, e.g. densely populated areas of Java, India, Mynmar in Asia form a poor market for luxury goods. On the other hand, densely populated areas along with high purchasing power create a large market, e.g. the West European countries and eastern U.S.A. Industrial products find outlets in such markets and hence many of the industries are set up near these areas in order to save the transportation costs of the final product.

- Industries manufacturing perishable goods are always located near the market, e.g. bakeries. Industries which require constant contacts .with consumers are also market oriented in their location, such as a printing press and the garment manufacturing industries. Sometimes, the final. product in the industries is fragile, hence such industries develop in markets, e.g. manufacturing chinaware. Certain industries are non-weight losing non-perishable raw material, e.g cotton textiles requires the light, non-weight losing raw material of cotton. Such industries usually develop near the market. Industries like those which manufacture electronic goods and plastics require raw material in small quantities. These plants also develop near the market as the cost of transporting the raw material to the plants is not high. Certain manufacturing, plants manufacture articles that are cheap in value but are bulky. Such final products involve high transportation costs hence are mainly located near the markets, e.g. plants manufacturing tiles or bricks.

- Thus, the nature of the raw materials and the final products together with the mark affect the location of the industries.

(5) Land :

- The majority of the industries require level land and hence they are mainly located in the plains. Mountainous areas do not attract industries due to inadequate raw materials and transportation facilities. If the industries are located in the valleys of mountainous areas, they do not get additional space for further expansion. e.g. some iron and steel industries of the U. S. A. were established in the Upper Ohio region in the valleys. Now they suffer from lack of room for expansion in the narrow valleys near Pittsburgh. That is why nowadays modern industrial development is concentrated along the shores of the Five Great lakes. Some factories require large areas. Such industries usually occupy non-agricultural land which lies away from the urban centres. Such lands are cheap and provide-ideal sites for industries.

(6) Labour :

- All manufacturing industries require an adequate labour, force. Availability of labour affects the location of industries in the following ways :

(a) Industries that require a large labour force always develop in areas of dense population. Such areas in developed countries provide skilled and semi-skilled labour, while such areas in developing countries provide a large pool of unskilled labour. Eastern U. S. A. and Western Europe are developed and prosperous regions which have technicians, scientists and skilled labour. Very few industries are developed in sparsely populated ares like the Asiatic part of Russian Federation and Western Australia.

(b) Some industries require highly skilled labour, e.g. diamond cutting. Such industries always come up in the developed areas. Antwerp and Amsterdam in Europe are famous for their diamond cutting industries.

(c) Some industries require a large unskilled, cheap labour force, e.g. cotton textile industries. These industries were among the first ones to be started in the developing countries where such labour is available.

(d) Highly skilled labourers are mobile. They get good jobs and attractive remunerations and hence can migrate to any region with better job opportunities. But, unskilled labourers are always poorly paid and cannot usually migrate to other regions.

(e) Strong unionized labourers continuously go on strike, demand higher wages and thus become troublesome to industries. Hence, new industries are normally set up outside such areas, e.g. due to the strongly unionized labourers in Maharashtra, new industries have started in Gujarat and Madhya Pradesh.

(7) Capital :

- A large amount of capital is required to set up industries. This capital is required to purchase land, machinery, raw materials; to construct the workshop and other buildings; to pay the wages of the workers and other staff, to pay, corporation tax, sales tax, income tax, excise tax and several other expenses. Naturally if other factors are available, industries come up in areas where this capital is available. Such finance is provided by the Government, private investors or large companies.

- But today capital does not require national boundaries. The prosperous and developed countries are always willing to give financial assistance to the developing countries of the world to set up their industries. Tin mining and smelting in Malaysia is carried out with the help of foreign capital. Several developed countries have provided capital to set up iron and steel industries in India.
- But these investors always take precautions before investing their money. They usually are not ready to invest in those countries which have political instability and where there is danger of nationalization.

(8) Technology :

- Development in manufacturing is not possible without technical knowledge. This is required to tap minerals from the mines, to manufacture machinery required for various factories e.g. to manufacture components of automobiles and so on. Thus, industries usually grow in areas having this technical know-Mw. Due to lack of technical knowledge, the undeveloped countries do not make progress in the field of manufacturing. In many cases, such countries rely on foreign experts and technology. Usually industries have developed in those areas where inventions were first made. e.g. the U. K., New England region of the U. S. A.

3.1.5 Geographical Influence Upon Business :

- The suitability to the chosen target market and accessibility of the business are substantially affected by the geographical influences.
- The ease of access which the business provides to the consumers is a significant effect of geographical influences.
- If it is convenient to access a business, the more consumers will be attracted to it for purchasing the product the business is selling.
- It demonstrates the great impact which external factors regarding geographical influences have upon businesses.
- **Accessibility :** Extent to which a consumer or user can obtain a good or service at the time is it needed.
- **Target Market :** A particular group of consumers at which a product or service is aimed.
- **Population growth :** It is an increase in number of people that reside in a country, state or city.
- **Global network :** A network composed of different interconnected networks that cover an unlimited geographical area.
- Businesses need to constantly monitor their environment in order to appeal to consumers.

The Importance of Location in Business

- Positioning of a business has always been an important element of establishing a business. Your success as a business depends on how well you are positioned to be found, which includes various factors from location to the price of your product or service to the message you use to promote the business, online and offline.

- The importance of the location of your business cannot be stressed enough, despite the rise of technology, virtual communication and cloud businesses. A business's address is an important factor in the way that business is perceived.
- If your business distant is from your target audience, especially if you sell offline, prospects may find it difficult to locate you. Conversely, if you had location at a place which is well-regarded as a business centre, prospects may be more.

(i) The best location can increase brand visibility :

- Location can also influence a business's ability to market itself, the competition it faces from businesses, the total cost of operation, taxes the business owner has to pay and the regulations they must follow.
- Location also matters for marketing. The importance of location goes beyond your business' physical location and your website rank in Google search results. It extends to the placement of your advertisements.
- For example, choosing a business address in the City of London will likely change the perception of your business as it would be seen to be part of the finance and high growth culture of the area. In the UK, Pall Mall Estates has workshop space available in a number of major cities, including London, Bournemouth, Birmingham, and Wellingborough.

(ii) Easy access is a huge advantage :

- Basically, you just want to be wherever your customers are and make it as convenient as possible to visit you. Location is of utmost importance especially to businesses that sell goods or services directly to customers at brick-and-mortar establishments.
- Some customers choose to buy from certain companies because of the perception they have about them. A business in the commercial area of a city gives the perception that the business is successful and can afford a good location.
- Your business should also consider if parking is available for prospective customers. Many customers will choose to go somewhere else if it's too hard to find parking.

(iii) Think about suppliers :

- Depending on your business, suppliers could influence your location. Price and quality are pre-requisites in choosing a supplier, but the speed of delivery has a huge impact on productivity.
- For better and quicker businesses operations, it's important to consider the location of your company to make it easy for your suppliers to reach your premises on time to deliver goods and provide the necessary service for your business to run smoothly. And the closer you are to your suppliers, the quicker your product can be on the market.
- Location will always be important especially for many businesses despite the rise of remote work, collaboration, telecommuting and virtual offices.
- If your business is conveniently located at the best place to attract customers, you can be certain of growth, an increase in sales and brand visibility.

- If you're running a traditional or physical business, your success primarily depends on your location. Do your research and choose your location carefully.
- Think about the following dynamics when choosing the location of your new business or when you plan on expanding to other cities.
  - Your business image
  - The competition you will face
  - Growth plans today and tomorrow
  - The overall safety and perception of the location
  - Laws and regulations

3.2   LOCATION - NEED AND IMPORTANCE

3.2.1   Ideal Location of Factory/Plant

(a) Ideal Location of Factory / Plant (Meaning) : In setting up a factory, a manufacturer has to take three inter-related decisions simultaneously.

  (i)   The scale of operation.

  (ii)   The technique to be adopted while selecting appropriate combination of factors of production.

  (iii) The location of the factory.

The conventional theory of the firm provides the rules or norms for the first two types of decisions to be taken. But it ignores the third one completely.

(b) Locational Decision Making : A separate branch of economics bordering with the discipline of geography, which is known as 'Industrial Location' or 'Locational Analysis' deals with the elements of the locational decision-making.

(c) Decision Making not Simple : The task of decision-making about industrial location is not very simple. A manufacturer has to consider several technical, economical and institutional factors. Location of industries means the methods and desirability of concentrating industries in different areas or localities. Further, each manufacturer has to find out from time to time whether favourable conditions still continue for the location of an industry.

Each industrialist will try to locate his unit at a place where the cost of production is lowest. This is called location of industries. On the other hand, when the industries are concentrated in a particular area, it is called localisation of industries which can be due to main reasons including physical location, availability of raw materials, labour etc. In short, locating a business involves relatively a large permanent investment. If the selection is improper, the manufacturer incurs a heavy loss. Thus, the site has to be carefully selected, that which may provide maximum advantage.

(d) Stages of Location : The problem of site selection of a factory can be solved in the following three stages :

(1) Selection of the region.

(2) Selection of the locality.

(3) Selection of actual site.

(1) Selection of the Region : Normally, the geographical area is divided on the basis of natural regions or political boundaries within the nation. For instance, Maharashtra State, Uttar Pradesh State etc. which region is suitable for location will be considered on the basis of comparative cost advantage.

(2) Selection of the Locality : Next to the selection of region, follows the selection of specific locality within the region. While selecting the locality following options are there –

(i) Urban area.

(ii) Rural area.

(iii) Sub-urban area.

The comparative advantages of each locality are considered at this stage.

(3) Selection of Actual Site : While making decisions on the selection of site certain facilities and factors have to be considered. For instance the type of development of land, cost of levelling, possibility of plant expansion, availability of infrastructural facilities like banking, power, communication, postal services etc.

3.2.2 Need for Balanced Regional Development of Industries

Following are the reasons for the need for balanced regional development of industries :

(a) **Development and Conservation of Resources :** "The aim of regional development should be to secure maximum efficiency in the utilisation of available resources. The setting up of different industries lead to fuller utilisation and conservation of mineral, agriculture and human resources of the region."

(b) **Maintaining Political Stability :** The regional disparities in income and wealth are the greatest danger to the national solidarity.

(c) **Overcoming Social Evils :** Localisation of industries in big towns and cities result in overcrowding, congestion and noise which affects the health and efficiency of inhabitants adversely.

(d) **Fast Development of the Economy :** Balanced regional development is pre-requisite for rapid development of the economy because the progress of the entire economy depends upon the development of all regions. The growth rates in different regions of the economy reflects the progress of the entire economy.

(e) **Smooth Development of the Economy :** If all the regions are equally developed, they may be helpful to each other and on the other hand, if there are regional inequalities, the less developed regions will retard the development.

(f) **Employment Opportunities :** The dispersal of industries in various regions not only helps in promoting the infrastructure in backward region but also in providing employment opportunities which in turn increase their per capita output and income.

(g) Minimizing Backwash Effects : The developing countries are characterized by regional differences in income and unemployment and the main cause of regional inequality is the strong backwash effects and the weak spread effects of such economies.

(II) Measures :

(a) Liberal issue of licenses on a preferential basis for starting industries in less developed regions.

(b) Establishment of industrial estates in all the states and special emphasis on small scale industries to bring about better regional distribution of industries.

(c) The central assistance to state for development of their backward areas.

(d) Location of central projects in the backward states.

(e) Large scale rural electrification.

(f) Provision of power, water and finance for backward regions at concessional rates.

(g) Provision of special training facilities in underdeveloped regions.

(h) Infrastructure facilities which are required by the industries in the underdeveloped areas.

3.2.3 Weber's theory of Industrial Location

(1) Weber's Theory of Industrial Location :

- Alfred Weber, a German economist has developed one of the earliest approaches to explain the location of manufacturing industry.

- Weber's main interest was to construct a general theory of location which could be applied to all industries at all times. For this, he took into consideration the general factors of location which were relevant to all industries. The factors were divided into two categories :

(a) Those influencing inter-regional location of industries i.e. regional factors.

(b) Those influencing inter-regional location i.e. agglomerating factors.

(2) Weber's analysis is based on certain assumptions :

(a) The locations of raw materials including fuel are fixed.

(b) Situation and size of consuming centres are given.

(c) There are several fixed labour supply centres. Labour is immobile and unlimited in supply at fixed wage rate.

(d) The institutional factors like taxation, interest, insurance, etc. are insignificant locational factors.

(e) The economic culture and political system are treated to be uniform and stable across the locations.

Thus, Weber assumed perfect competition for his model.

(3) Locational Figure :

- Weber found three general factors which vary regionally (i.e. differ from region to region) raw material costs, transport costs and labour costs.
  Weber started his analysis with the proposition that a manufacturing unit tends to locate at the place where cost of transportation is minimum.

He used the 'locational triangle' of Launhardt to find the place of minimum transport cost.

- According to **Weber**, the fundamental factors which determine transport costs are weight of the goods to be transported and the distance to be covered. According to this theory, every industry has a 'location figure' of least transportation cost consisting of points of raw materials deposits and consumption centres.

- Therefore, an industry may be material-oriented or market-oriented from location point of view. Weber used the 'Material Index' for identifying such nature of the industry. The Material Index (MI) is defined as –

$$MI = \frac{\text{Weight of Localised Material}}{\text{Weight of Finished Product}}$$

(4) Classification of Materials :

The material index formula is simplified by Weber.

According to his theory, raw materials are grouped as :

(a) Localised materials which are confined to certain localities e.g. minerals, raw jute, wood pulp etc.

(b) Natural raw materials which are generally available everywhere e.g. water, clay etc.

Thus, the former exerts greater pressure in influencing location of an industry than the second group. However, the theory points out that all localised raw materials do not attract industries to their centres to the same extent. Localised raw materials can be further categorized as :

(a) Pure Materials like cotton, wool, raw jute which do not lose weight in the process of production.

(b) Gross Materials which are weight losing e.g. coal. It is better to have the manufacturing unit at the place of deposit of weight losing materials as transport costs involved in shifting raw materials which is lost in the process of production would be saved.

- **Deducing** from the above considerations, the industrial unit will be located at a place where transport costs are minimum.

(5) Causes of Deviation of Location :

- However, industries may not be necessarily centred at the point of minimum transport costs as the entrepreneur is interested not just in transport costs but in total costs. Thus, there may be deviation of an industry from the location where transport costs are least because another place is more favourable from point of labour supply.

- Weber states, "A location can be moved from the point of minimum transportation costs to more favourable labour location only if savings in cost of labour are larger than additional cost of transportation".

In respect of labour costs as a point to attract industries, two factors are important :

(a) The labour cost index, which is the ratio between cost of labour per ton product.

(b) The locational weight, which is total weight to be transported during the whole process of production.

- According to **Weber**, the extent of variation caused varying labour costs is determined by ratio between 'labour cost index' and 'labour coefficient' i.e. ratio between labour cost index and locational weight.

Thus, comes the second rule in Weber's theory :

- "When labour costs are varied, an industry deviates from its transport locations in proportion to the size of its labour coefficient."
- Weber also examined the possibility of more than one site of location for an industry. This is **split in location.** This is when different stages of production in any industry can be carried on independently and at different places. e.g. paper industry, where pulp is made near the forests while the paper is manufactured near the market i.e. consumption centre.

(6) Criticism :

- Weber's theory of industrial location is severely criticised by a number of economists such as **Sargent Florence, Andreas Predohl, A. Robinson** on various grounds as follows :

(a) Sargent Florence is a critic of the purely deductive approach of Weber. He states that vague generalisations cannot provide suitable answers to the theory of location of industries, because number of non-economic factors influence location of an industry.

(b) Sargent Florence also points out to the unrealistic assumptions. Weber, while analysing labour orientation, has made two assumptions fixed labour centres and unlimited supply of labour. But these assumptions of Weber are not correct because a rise of an industry at a place may create new labour centres and it is also incorrect to assume unlimited supply at any centre.

(c) In a competitive market structure, it would not be true to assume fixed points of consumption. It is invalid assumption because consumers are spread all over the country and not concentrated at fixed centres. A. Robinson expresses that consumption centres are both the cause and effect of location of an industry.

(d) S. R. Dennison criticises Weber's theory on the ground that it is overburdened with technical considerations. He says, Weber's theory is only in terms of technical coefficient, cost and the price find no place in this theory. In fact, an economist's analysis should be based mainly on considerations of costs and price.

Weber's Theory of Industrial Location (With Criticism) Economics :

- Alfered Weber a German economist was the first economist who gave scientific exposition to the theory of location and thus filled a theoretical gap created by classical economists. He gave his ideas in his Theory of Location of Industries' which was first published in German language in 1909 and translated into English in 1929. His theory, which is also known as 'Pure Theory' has analytical approach to the problem.
- The basis of his theory is the study of general factors which pull an industry towards different geographical regions. It is thus deductive in approach. In his theory he has taken into consideration factors that decide the actual setting up of an industry in a particular area.

Weber's Problems :

- Weber was faced with many serious problems. He wanted to find out why did industry moved from one place to another and what factors determined the movement. After considerable thinking he came to the conclusion that causes be responsible for this migration could be Regional Factors Primary Causes and Agglomerative and deglomerative factors (Secondary Factors).
- In so far as regional factors were concerned these, among other things, included cost of the ground, buildings, machines, material, power, fuel, labour, transportation charges and amount of interest that the capital would have earned.

(i) Regional Factors (Primary Causes) :

- According to Weber transportation costs play a vital role in the location of an industry. Each industry will try to find location at a place where transportation charges are the barest minimum, both in terms of availability of resources and place of consumption. According to him transportation costs are determined by the weight to be transported on the one hand and distance to be covered on the other.
- Then the cost will also depend on the type of transportation system available and the extent to which it is in use. the nature of the region i.e. whether rocky, plain, connected or unconnected with roads etc. the kinds of the roads in the area where the goods are to be transposed; nature of facilities required i.e. whether the goods are to be taken with great care, less care or even without any special care.

Locational Figure :

- While discussing regional factors, Weber has discussed the idea of locational figure. According to him every industry will try to see that it is located at a place where raw material is available nearest to the place of consumption on the one hand and most advantageously located material deposits on the other. According to Weber, "Thus locational figures are created. These locational figures, therefore, represent the first and most important basis for formulating the theory."

Classification of Material :

Weber, before proceeding further, has classified raw material into different categories e.g. :

(a) Ubiquities material; which is suitable everywhere e.g. bricks, clay etc., and

(b) Localised material e.g., iron ore, mineral etc. which is available in certain regions and not everywhere. Obviously the later play a bigger and important role than the former. He has also categorised raw material as 'Pure' and 'Weight Losing' raw material is one which impart its whole weight to the products e.g. cotton, wool etc. and weight losing materials are those in which only a part of the material enters into the weight.

Laws of Transportation :

- Weber, while discussing the theory of location, has also discussed laws of transportation. According to him material index measures the total weight to be moved. From material index he understood the portion of the weight of localised material to the weight of the product. According to him, "All industries whose material index is not greater than one and whose locational weight therefore, are not greater than two lie at the place of consumption."

Causes of Deviation of Location :

- Weber was faced with a serious problem namely why the industries deviate from the centre of least transport costs. One such reason could be differences in the labour costs. This labour cost can be cheap either because of differing levels of efficiency and of wages of labour or because of differing levels of efficiency in the organisation and the technical equipment which the labour is required to use. Labour cost can go up and come down due to distribution of population as well.

- But whatsoever might be the reason for the low labour cost, According to Prof Kuchhal, deviation "will be possible only when the additional cost of transportation at the new centre is more than compensated by a saving in labour costs... When the labour costs are varied, an industry deviates from its transport locations in proportion to the size of its labour co-efficient".

- Weber himself has said that, with a high index of labour costs, a large quantity of labour costs will be available for comparison with correspondingly high critical isodapanes, and therefore we shall find a high potential attracting powers of the labour locations and vice versa.

- According to Weber's theory if the behaviour of each industry in respect of labour cost is to be measured than it is necessary to calculate the proportion of labour costs per ton of weight to be moved.

(ii) Agglomerative and Deglomerative Factory (Secondary Causes) :

- We have so far been discussing primary causes of industrial location. Weber has also discussed secondary causes responsible for industrial location. He has taken into account agglomerative and deglomerative factors. An agglomerative factor, according to him is a factor which provides an advantage in production or marketing a commodity simply because industry is located at one place. On the other hand deglomerative factor is one which gives such advantage because of decentralisation of production.

- Agglomerative factors include gas, water etc. and are conducive for concentration of industry and deglomerative factors include land values and taxes and lead to decentralisation. Pulls of agglomerative factors are index of manufacture and locational weight. According to Weber ratio of manufacturing cost of locational weight is co-efficient of manufacture.

- According to Weber Agglomeration is encouraged with high co-efficient and deglomeration with low. According to him, We shall do well to bear in mind that labour orientation is one form of deviation from the minimum point; agglomeration to another.

- When agglomerative forces appear in an industry oriented towards labour, there takes place a competition between the agglomerative deviation and the labour deviation, a struggle to create, locations for agglomeration, as compared with labour locations, both bearing upon the foundations of the transportational ground work.

Split in Location :

- Weber has considered the possibility of location of an industry at more than open one, particularly when production in an industry can be carried independently at more than one place. According to him in fact single location is an exception and split a rule. It is essential, according to him that all productive processes must go on at one and the same place and it is better that these be carried out at different stages and at number of places. Split is to occur in two stages. In the first stage it is elimination of waste and in the second working up of pure material.

Locational Coupling :

- Weber along with split in location has also given the idea of locational coupling, meaning thereby that different types of industries can be coupled in one and the same locality. According to him it is just possible to combine production of different articles in one plant because of the availability of several raw materials from the same source.

- This coupling can be possible either due to economic or technical reasons. It is also possible due to connection through material e.g., if the byproduct of one industry happens to be raw material for another then the two industries may select a single place of location. Locational coupling can also be due to market connection between two industries. In such a case product of one industry may enter into another industry without being used as material or half finished product.

Criticism of Weber's Theory :

- Weber's Theory of Industrial location has been put to several criticisms.

(1) Unrealistic Assumptions :

- According to critics of this theory, Weber has unrealistically over-simplified the theory of industrial location. Many assumptions in the theory are unrealistic. According to them Weber has taken only two elements for determining the cost of transportation namely weight and distance. He has not given due to place to the type of transport, quality of goods to be transported, topography, character of region etc.

(2) Labour Centres Notion Defective :

- Weber's ideas about labour centres have also not been accepted. He has started with the presumption that there are fixed labour centres with unlimited supplies of labour in each of them. Obviously both these assumptions are not correct. There cannot be fixed labour centres, because each industry creates new labour centres. Similarly there can never be unlimited supplies of labour in any centre.

(3) Ideas about Fixed Points of Consumption :

- It is argued that Weber's idea does not work well with the market conditions in a competitive structure. Consumers are always scattered all over the country and thus consumer centres always shift with a shift in industrial population. There can therefore be no fixed point of consumption.

(4) Vague Generalisations :

- Weber, while expounding his theory of industrial location, it is believed, certain vague generalisations. He has given no due place to non-economic factors of industrial location, which play a big role in this regard. Who can deny that there are certain historical and social forces which go a long way while deciding industrial location of an industry, but he has completely ignored them, which has made his theory very unrealistic.

(5) Not a Deductive Theory :

- Andreas Predohl is of the view that Weber's Theory is only selective and not deductive. According to him he has made an artificial distinction between general and special factors which influence location of an industry. Such a distinction, in fact, has no logical significance. According to Weber transport costs and labour costs are only general costs. He has failed to explain why capital costs and management costs cannot be included or covered under it.

(6) Defective Method of Analysis :

- Weber has tried to classify material into ubiquities and fixed material. Again the division is arbitrary. According to Robinson who does not know that in actual practice materials are drawn from a large number of alternative fixed points.

(7) Overburdened with Technical Considerations :

- Dennison is of the view that Weber's theory is heavily over burdened with technical considerations. It has not laid due stress on costs and prices and has over stressed technical coefficients. According to him, "The most important criticism about Weber's analysis is that it is lamentably removed from all considerations of costs and prices and it is formulated mainly in terms of technical coefficients."

Utility of the Theory :

- No doubt theory suffers from some serious defects, yet it cannot be denied that it has its own value, importance and significance. It is primarily because the alternatives given are neither comprehensive nor complete. So far it is the only theory which is capable of universal application.
- Andreas Predohl has also given his ideas about industrial location and has come to the conclusion that every change of industrial location involves a change in the combination of means of production. But this theory obviously does not provide any guidelines for locating new industries.

3.2.4 New Balanced Approach Theory of Industrial Location

New Balanced Approach Theory of Industrial Location :

(a) Prominent Economists : The economists like Ohlin, Losch, Palander and others particularly during recent years have given their attention towards industrial location.

(b) Interest in the Study of Locational Dynamics : The ever increasing interest in the study of locational dynamics has been mainly attributed for analysing the present frame-work of industrial orientation as well as for formulating a realistic policy of locational planning in the best interests of balanced regional economic growth of a country.

(c) Urgent Need : Policy makers feel that there is an urgent need for some kind of regional planning of industry which should aim at maximum efficiency of an industrial unit and lead to an optimum distribution of industrial activity based on broader economic, social and strategical objectives. The reconciliation of these apparently incompatible objectives is found to be very important due to :

(i) The change in position and functions of the government with regard to the economic system.

(ii) The growing disposition to look beyond narrow profit and loss considerations to the broader welfare aspects.

(iii) The consequent demand for more conscious economic planning at the highest, national level.

(d) Broader Considerations : It is very clear that the study of locational dynamics should not be nominated by limited economic consideration alone, but be based on broader economic, social and strategical considerations too.

3.3   LIMITATIONS TO LOCAL LOCALIZATION PROCESS AND SOURCING OF LOCATION

3.3.1 Localisation of Industries

- Localisation means the concentration of certain industry in a particular area, locality or region, localisation is related to the territorial division of labour, that is specialisation by areas and regions.

Advantage of Localization of Industries :

- There are many benefits which an industry derives by becoming localised at a certain location.

These advantages may be summarized as follows :

(i) Labour gets trained because dexterity and skill are handed down from one generation of labourers to the next and a large body of trained labour is built up.

(ii) A large market for a particular type of labour is developed in a locality. Labour of this type can migrate to that locality where there is almost a sure guarantee of employment. Employers in search of labour of this type can also find it there.

(iii) Financial facilities develop and banks are started there. The industry enjoys the benefit of cheap credit facilities.

(iv) Suitable means of communication and transport develops. This is a great advantage to the localised industry.

(v) Subsidiary or supplementary industries develop and provides a wider range of employment for labour and capital. The by-products are put to economical uses.

(vi) The reputation of a locality for particular goods widens the market. Orders flow in from distant places. It is a assured market. The industry can have a steady growth.

(vii) Technical journals are published, Training and research institutes are established from which the industrialists benefit a great deal.

(viii) It brings prosperity to the locality and provides employment and adds to the income of the people.

(ix) Collective action is rendered possible because the industrialists organise themselves in associations to safeguard their common interests, and so do the labourers.

(x) Several improvements are made in the industry, because there is opportunity for exchange of ideas. There is healthy rivalry. All this is beneficial for the industry.

Disadvantages of Localizations of Industries:

- Localization of industries has it's disadvantages. Several evils are associated with it.

(i) **Scope of employment is restricted :** Employment is available for one type of labour only. In a centre, where there is a greater variety of employment, the entire family of a worker may find employment. But here only a few of them will get work so that the total family income remain low.

(ii) **Dependence on the main industry is risky :** A depression in a particular industry is bound to spell disaster to the whole locality.

(iii) **Over-specialisation leads to dependence :** on other centres which proves very dangerous in times of war. We may not be able to import the necessary materials and machinery. Dependence on foreign markets for the disposal of goods is also risky.

(iv) **The dishonesty :** of a few manufacturers brings into disrepute all the rest. The products of the locality get a bad name, and even honest manufacturers suffer.

- **It leads to over-congestion.** This seriously tells upon the health and efficiency of workers and their children. This is what has happened in Mumbai, Calcutta, Kanpur, etc.

(v) **Labour tends to lose its mobility for obvious reasons :** They have to be content to remain where they are. There are few other openings in the locality.

(vi) **Risk of attack.** Bombing during a war may paralyse the industry. Hence there is a lack of security. The big industrial cities are the usual targets of the enemy attack.

3.4 RURAL AND HANDICRAFT INDUSTRIES - ECONOMIC AND COMMERCIAL IMPORTANCE

Rural Industry in India

- In rural areas, there are many industries, i.e. agriculture, forest, and handloom industries. People living in different areas of rural India have unique skills. i.e. the rural people living in Kerala, have professional skill in carving wood, the other rural people proficient in weaving carpet live in Kashmir.

- In India, the agriculture is very important for the economy because it accounts for a significant part of GDP it offers nearly 55% of rural employment.

- A rural enterprise refers to a company registered in the rural areas, under the Department for Environment, Food and Rural Affairs.

- Business operating in the rural areas due to favorable factors such as the dwelling, fresh air, good cheaper rental fees, and harmonious relationships with labor.
- There are nearly 90% of employees are residents who work in an assigned area in the countryside and aim to increase the local economy.
- The Mahatma Gandhi National Rural Employment Guarantee Act has been implemented to increase the opportunities for rural wage employment.

Types of rural industries :

(i) Agriculture Industries :

- The agriculture industry is very important as it solve the subsistence of the 2/3 of the population in the field study at Ambedkar Nagar district, in which, the labor force of India accounts for 52%, and this sector made the contribution of 15.7% of the Gross domestic product between 2008 and 2009.
- The majority of the national economy is contributed by the agricultural industry. The job of people who lived in rural India is still mainly in agricultural. Nevertheless, it also found that the agricultural has a receding proportion in the GDP.
- There are approximately 91% of the population in the 13 selected villages (Studied) in India works associated with farming, among these, over 86% are the small and marginal farmers who have an achievement of cultivating 75% of the total arable land. Besides, the agrarian economy mainly comes from the little area and marginal and small land possessed by farmers.
- The sources or crops that can generate incomes and trying to satisfy the need of the consumers is needed to sustain their daily life. For example, the commercial products (milk, vegetables, and fruits) are the sources that can be traded in markets and are required by the residents as secured food.
- The small and medium farmers are more likely to foster diversified resources with catering the demand such as the grains, fibers, and oilseeds, which makes more profits.
- Thus many farmers made a transformation from farm to non-farm agriculture businesses. For instance, there are roughly 66% of the peasant engaged in non-traditional agricultural enterprises.

(ii) Forest Industries :

- The forest industry traditionally produces two primary resources, which are timber and non-timber forest products (NTEPs). The fuelwood plays a crucial role among the forest products as it for example taking up more than 35% average forest income in the selected 27 villages around the Jharkhand in India. Besides, the forest income is significant because it made 12% to 42% increases to the village economy, and it is the dominant source of income in HFLA and HFHA villages. It is using the majority of the firewood in the rural family as a source for heating in the selected villages in Jharkhand, thus, less than 10% of the fuelwood for trading. Apart from the firewood, there is another forest product also very valuable, which is NTFPs. The timber uses for producing furniture and equipment.

- In contrast, the NTFPs encompass the products that can use in different areas, such as the medicinal plants for healing, some specific plants used in making cosmetics.
- Therefore, the function of the NTFPs also can be related to religion, not merely on the trade and the products.

(iii) Handloom industries :

- The handloom industries in Odisha is followed by the agriculture sector in terms of the contribution of the employment, which maintained the livelihood of the weavers. The Bastralaya handloom cooperative produces traditional clothes (sarees, lungis) and household's products (bed cover) with dyeing yarns.
- Furthermore, there is a complicated braid art called Ikat, which has prominent patterns on the silk with using environmentally friendly colored threads.
- Should possess textile skills, learn new knowledge through regular activities and observe the needs of the customer such as the color they prefer for the sarees, these competencies with the help of Bastralaya company will improve social-economic conditions. In this manner, the Bastralaya commit to bringing more earnings for weavers.

Structure of rural enterprise :

- A Joint family enterprise in India has a dominant place due to the concept of family and the incentives of the economic benefits. The Joint family encompasses two types of family, which are patrilineal and matrilineal.
- The partnership between members or relatives with the same caste and sub-caste will bring significant start-up capital and assistance to solve the issue, such as handling all of the business simultaneously.
- **For example,** 23 partnership ventures have a corporation with family members in the total of the 48 enterprises in the selected two villages at Gujarat.
- It could also happen that the partnership is established outside of the joint family.

Rural enterprise in India :

- In India, there are different forms of rural enterprises, which are community-based organizations, self-help groups, and cooperatives, these companies are beneficial for the rural economy due to the job opportunities created.
- There are some challenges for enterprise in rural India, i.e. limited assets, inadequate skills and labors, unsteady communication system, and weak transport infrastructure.
- The deficit of knowledge on promoting the product may lead to the proposition of improper decisions.
- Anand Milk Union limited is an India dairy cooperative; it applied the e-business in rural India to gain a robust supply chain, eliminate transport obstacles, and have a good relationship with customers.

Rural Cooperatives in India :

- Cooperatives in India are one of the most extensive system in terms of rural finance in the world. Agricultural cooperatives in India have excellent scope for improvement with the changing economy.

- By reaching a large number of clients, farmers (small and marginal farmers), and people under the poverty line, it can be seen that rural cooperatives have an essential role in the hinterland of rural area. There are approximately 4.5 lakh cooperatives in India with 220 million people involved.
- Cooperatives originated from the twentieth century, and these cooperatives at an early stage mainly catered to the financial needs of the farmer, especially during the advent of harvesting and sowing. Today, the cooperatives are responsible for the majority of the rural credit, which constituted for 65%.
- Under the cooperatives system in India, the credit cooperative is a powerful system in India, which encompasses the organization of rural credit cooperative.
- The other types of cooperatives found are societies of farmer service and multipurpose society for large-scale agricultural activities. Rural cooperatives also engaged in distributing quality inputs to farmers by charging maximum price through the activity of procurement.
- The dairy cooperatives in rural India helps women involved in the production of the milk and acquiring confidence, more specifically, concerning the success of the Amul experiment.
- Pravaranagar Cooperative Sugar Industry is a successful example as far as the contribution to the development of the social-economic conditions about increasing the economic benefit and the improvement of the rural facilities, which are inclusive of the areas of education, recreation center, hospitals, and cooperatives.

Rural Self-Help Groups (SHG's) :

- The self-help group in India is active in a wide range, which helps approximately 33 million of Indian women to obtain financial services and other activities with lower prices.
- Women in rural India, especially with lower castes and lower education level, facing a plight such as the adverse health condition and limitation to acquire financial products. There are commonly 10 to 20 members in a rural self-help group, who funded money mutually for the enterprise or emergency.
- In Tamil Nadu, India new self-help groups were established after the natural disaster.
- One of the famous models launched in rural India is to provide microcreditto poor Indian women. The initiatives of rural development in India concentrate on the development of the economic status of women and other vulnerable people.
- Besides, there is another model not which only offer the Microfinance plus but also involved in the areas of education, social attendance, and politics. The self-help group has ethical implications for Indian women, such as alleviating the economic burden and eliminating gender inequality.
- There has been improvement for rural women in the aspects of psychological and economic conditions. Moreover, women who are widowed will receive support. In South India, the large proportion of rural women, especially widows, experienced poverty, uncertainty in the inheritance of land, and barriers of involving in community.

- The existence of the rural self-help group is to empower the vulnerable group, especially women, to conquer the barriers

Handicraft :

- A handicraft, refers to artisanal handicraft or handmade products, of a wide variety types of work useful and decorative objects are made completely by hand or by using only simple tools.
- It is a traditional craft, and applies to a wide range of creative and design activities that are related to making things with one's hands and skill, including work with textiles, moldable and rigid materials, paper, plant fibers, etc.
- One of the world's oldest handicraft is Dhokra; this is a sort of metal casting that has been used in India for over 4,000 years.
- Collective terms for handicrafts include artisanry, handicrafting, crafting, handcraftsman-ship and handcrafting. The term arts and crafts is also applied, especially in the United States and mostly to hobbyists' and children's output rather than items crafted for daily use, but this distinction is not formal.
- Handicrafting has its roots in the rural crafts—the material-goods necessities—of ancient civilizations, and many specific crafts have been practiced for centuries, while others are modern inventions, or popularizations of crafts which were originally practiced in a limited geographic area.
- The individual artisanship of a handicrafted item is the paramount criterion; those made by mass production or machines are not handicraft goods.
- Seen as developing the skills and creative interests of students, generally and sometimes towards a particular craft or trade, handicrafts are often integrated into educational systems, both informally and formally.
- Handicraft output often has cultural and/or religious significance, and increasingly may have a political message as well as in craftivism.
- Many crafts become very popular for brief periods of time (a few months, or a few years), spreading rapidly among the crafting population as everyone emulates the first examples.

Small Scale Industries Definition :

- Previously, the definition of small scale industries depended upon the business's capital and labour. This definition is still used to demarcate between small, medium and large-scale industries.
- The Central Government has the authority to determine capital investment requirements for small-scale industries. These requirements are listed under the Industries (Development and Regulation) Act, 1951.
- A small enterprise in which investment in plant & machinery ranges between ₹ 25 lakhs to ₹ 5 crores is a small-scale industry.
- Similarly, for industries that provide services, the investment requirement is between ₹ 10 lakhs and ₹ 2 crores.

Role and importance of Small Scale Industries :

- Small scale industries help in increasing employment and economic development of India. It improves the growth of the country by increasing urban and rural growth.
- Role of Small and medium scale enterprises are to help the government in increasing infrastructures and manufacturing industries, reducing issues like pollution, slums, poverty, and many development acts.
- Small scale manufacturing industries and cottage industries play a very important role in the economic development of India. If any amount of capital is invested in small scale industries it will help in reducing unemployment in India and increasing self-employment. The industry is a sector in which the production of goods is a segment of the economy.

Role and Importance of Small Scale Industries

- Increases total exports
- Increases production
- Improves the employment rate
- Opens new opportunities
- Advances welfare

- Every small-scale industry plays a big role in the Indian economy. It provides employment to crores of people, it has the added benefit of minimum capital requirements. The government also offers several tax benefits to SSI for this purpose.
- They can exist in urban as well as rural areas. Small Scale Industries have been able to compete with large-scale industries and multinational corporations because of this.

The following are some specific roles that SSIs play in the Indian economy :

(1) Increases Production :

- These industries produce goods and services worth over ₹ 40 lakhs for every investment of ₹ 10 lakhs. Furthermore, the value addition in this output increases by over 10%.
- India is one of the world's fastest growing economies in the world. Consequently, its production output is massive. It is important to note that SSIs contribute almost 40% of India's gross industrial value.
- The number of Small Scale Industries in India increased from around 8 lakhs in 1980 to over 30 lakhs in 2000.
- This figure has grown even more in recent years owing to the government's 'Ease of Doing Business' policies.
- As a result of this, the total industrial production output rose significant in the last few years. SSIs are, therefore, strongly responsible for the growth of India's economy.

(2) Increases Export :

- Besides producing more goods and services, SSIs have done well in exports.
- Almost half of India's total exports these days come from small-scale businesses.
- 35% of the total exports account for direct exports by SSIs, while indirect exports amount to 15%.

- Even trading houses and merchants help SSIs export their goods and services to foreign countries.

(3) Improves Employment Rate :

- It is important to note that SSI's employs more people than all industries after agriculture.
- Nearly four individuals can get full employment if ₹ 10 lakhs are invested in fixed assets of small-scale sectors.
- SSIs employ people in urban as well as rural areas.
- It distributes employment patterns in all parts of the country and prevents unemployment crisis.

(4) SSI Open New Opportunities :

- Small-scale industries offer several advantages and opportunities for investments.
- i.e. they receive many tax benefits and rebates from the government. The opportunity to earn profits from SSIs are big due to many reasons.
- (i)   SSIs are less capital intensive. They even receive financial support and funding easily.
- (ii) Secondly, arranging manpower and raw materials is also relatively easier for them. Even the government's export policies favour them heavily.

(5) SSI Advances Welfare :

- Besides providing profitable opportunities, Small Scale Industries play a large role in advancing welfare measures in the Indian economy as well.
- A large number of poor and marginalized sections of the population depend on them for their sustenance.
- These industries not only reduce poverty and income inequality but they also increase the standards of living of poor people. At the same time they enable people to make a living with dignity.

Points to Remember

- Manufacturing is a secondary economic activity of man.
- The Industrial Revolution began in Europe and then spread to different parts of the world.
- Industrial Economics is a "term for economic analysis as applied to Industry".
- Factors affecting Industrial location :
    - **(I) Primary Factors :**
        - (a) Supply of Raw materials
        - (b) Nearness to Market
        - (c) Transport facilities
        - (d) Supply of location
        - (e) Power
        - (f) Supply of Capital
    - **(II) Secondary factors :**
        - (a) Natural Factors
        - (b) Historical and Religious factors

- (c) Entrepreneurship   (d) Personal factors
- (e) Strategic Considerations   (f) External Economics
- (g) Government Subsidies and facilities
- (h) Miscellaneous factors

- Role of Industries in Economic development
  - (i) Boosted the Primary sector
  - (ii) Development of Transportation
  - (iii) Important in the living standards
  - (iv) Benefited trade
  - (v) Self-sufficiency
  - (vi) Employment for excess population

- Role of Industries in India's economic development
  - (i) Generals employment   (ii) Economic growth
  - (iii) Agro-based Industries   (iv) Complementary progress
  - (v) Higher per capita income   (vi) Exploitation of resources
  - (vii) Foreign exchange   (viii) Balanced development
  - (ix) Self-sustained growth   (x) Nation's Security

- Factors affecting Industrial location :
  - **(1) Raw material :**
    - (a) Raw material
    - (b) Bulky and perishable raw materials
    - (c) Light, Non-weight losing raw materials
    - (d) Manufactured raw material
    - (e) Imported raw material
  - **(2) Power :**
    - (a) Coal   (b) Oil   (c) Electricity
  - (3) Transport
  - (4) Market
  - (5) Land
  - (6) Labour
  - (7) Capital
  - (8) Technology

- Alfred Weber, a Garman economist has developed one of the earliest approaches to explain the location of manufacturing industry.
- Localization
- Types of Rural Industries :
  - (i) Agriculture Industries   (ii) Forest Industries
  - (iii) Handloom Industries   (iv) Handicraft

- Role and importance of small scale industries :
  - (i) Increased production
  - (ii) Increased total exports
  - (iii) Improve the employment rate
  - (iv) Opens new opportunities
  - (v) Increase welfare

Questions for Discussion

1. Define Industrial Economics. What is the scope of Industrial Economics ?
2. What are the objectives of Industries Economics ?
3. What are the various factors affecting Industries location ?
4. What is the role of Industries in Economic development ?
5. What is the role of Industries in the economic development of India ?
6. What are the factors affecting Industrial Location ?
7. What is the importance of location in Business ?
8. What are the Advantages and Disadvantages of Localisation of Industries ?
9. What is the need for balanced regional development of Industries ?
10. State Weber's theory of Industrial Location.
11. What is the economic are commercial importance of Rural and Handicraft Industries ?
12. What are the types of Rural Industries ?
13. What is the role of Small Scale Industries ?

Chapter **4**...

Trade and Transportations (Global Context)

Contents ...

Learning Objectives ...

➢ To Study the modes are means of transportation for the progress of agricultural, mineral and Industrial resources.

➢ Understanding the importance of Trade centers for the trade at commercial activities of a nation.

➢ To Study in detail about the recent trends and various transportation modes and its role in the commercial activities undertake.

INTRODUCTION

Transport and communication is a major tertiary economic activity. It involves the movement of passengers and goods as well as communication media like radio, television, telephone, telegraph, postal system, and satellites. Transport and communication are the arteries of any region. They facilitate the flow of a variety of commodities, ideas and people from one place to another. The economic development of any region depends largely on the development of transport and communication.

Functions of transport :

1. Movement of goods :

This economic activity is founded on the basis of the certain variations found in the world. All areas in the world do not share same physiographical features, the same climate, the same soil and vegetation and the same other natural resources. Thus some areas produce certain commodities in excess while other areas are in short supply of these very commodities. Many a times, such areas of plenty lie far away from the areas of scarcity. Transport carries out the major function of delivering commodities from areas of production to the areas of consumption. This gives rise to national and international trade.

2. Movement of people :

Since historic times, people have been moving from one place to another place for various reasons. However, the large scale movement of people was made possible through the modern means of transportation. During the 18th and 19th centuries thousands of people could migrate from Europe to the new lands of America and Australia because of increased knowledge about navigation.

3. Diffusion of ideas :

Transport and communication plays an important role in the diffusion of ideas. People from different parts of the world can communicate easily with the help of wireless, telephones and satellites. More people are thus able to utilise the advances made in science and technology.

4.1 ROLE AND IMPORTANCE OF TRADE

4.1.1 Trade

- Trade is a tertiary occupation. Trade brings about exchange of goods between two regions. Such exchanges are important for man's progress. Since early times man has been indulging in exchange, although the type of exchange was different in the past. Things were exchanged directly. This was called the. barter system. Its form and intensity went changing with the passage of time, though earlier it did not have a set pattern, direction or a particular intensity. Simple commodities were exchanged, directly. As time changed, and science and technology improved the general conditions of man's living, the world became smaller and smaller and trade developed. With an increase in the amount and the types of transport and better storage facilities available, trade increased tremendously, both in its volume and in its variety. For this reason, certain regions of the world have started specialising in certain kinds of productions which have become totally export-oriented. The economic policy of certain other governments is totally import- oriented regarding certain commodities. It shows the importance and the ease with which trade takes place in the modern world.

- The level of trade can be. different. It can take place within a small region between two persons, between two states or between two countries. Give and take, or buying and selling between two parties at any level is called trade. The development of trade has the following bases :

(1) Unlimited wants : Man's wants. -demands and desires are unlimited. He is all the time looking around to tap the natural resources for his wants, comforts and luxuries. This leads to him getting even that product which is not found locally.

(2) Shortage of certain commodities : No region in the world is self-sufficient in the true sense. Trade takes place when there is a demand for a certain commodity in a region. Such need arises when there is a shortage of that commodity within the region. Such regions are ready to obtain that commodity from any region that has a surplus. For example, the tropical crops of tea, coffee, cocoa are not grown in the U. S. A. where mostly temperate conditions are found. But, they are required by the U. S. A. So they are imported from the tropical countries like India, Sri Lanka and Brazil.

(3) Surplus productions : Some regions of the world have a surplus production of certain commodities. Thus, a shortage in one region and a surplus in the other region leads to the flow of goods or trade. For example, in the Prairie region of the U. S. A. and Canada, there is an abundance of wheat resulting in a surplus which is taken to some of the eastern -countries e.g. to India to meet their food shortage. Similarly, Canada has a surplus of soft wood. She exports wood, pulp and paper to many countries of the world.

(4) Inter-regional or inter-country relations : If different regions or different countries have healthy relations between them, then only trade will be favoured between them. Various political factors plays their part in developing good or bad relations between countries. Only good relations can boost trade. For example, strained relations between Iran and Iraq have adversely affected trade between them. Similarly, strained relation between India and Pakistan has resulted in a meagre flow of goods between the two countries so far.

(5) Economic well-being : One region has to have the ability to buy the commodities from another region. This ability exists only if the region is economically well-off. The economic position should be stable enough to give it the required level of purchasing power, otherwise trade will not develop. West European countries and the U. S. A. are the leading" world traders. The reason behind this is their economic well-being.

- So, a shortage of certain commodities, surplus productions, unlimited wants, good relations and a good level of purchasing power are the bases for the presence and development of trade.

- Further, it is worthwhile noting the factors which give rise to these bases. They are the following :

(I) Geographical Environment :

- Geographical environment differs from region to region. This is the very basis of trade. Further, differences in geographical environment are present because of the differences in the following natural factors :

(a) Relief : Differences in relief affect the type of crops, vegetation, animals and the costs involved in the production of commodities. Some crops require sloping ground e.g. tea. As a result, it can be grown only in hilly regions, e.g. Assam Hills and Nilgiris in India and the slopes of the central massif in Sri Lanka. Similarly, to grow rice, low-lying level lands are better than any other region. 'The total rice production of Assam is not comparable to that of the low-lying areas of West Bengal. Therefore, only those regions which have the required relief characteristics can specialise in particular crops which, in turn, can result in a surplus production leading to trade ultimately. Further, mountains affect the distribution and amount of rainfall. Certain mountain slopes are clothed with luxurious forests while certain slopes are bare. This difference in forest products also can affect trade in these commodities. The southern, wet slopes of the state' of Jammu and Kashmir in India are favourable for timber production. Further, difficult relief (mountains, plateaus) is a barrier to the development of means of transport and this hinders trade, e.g. Jammu and Kashmir.

(b) Climate : Climate affects the following :

(i) Man's capacity and health : Certain climates are enervating e.g. in tropical Africa East Indies, Amazon basin where man feels lethargic and drained of energy due to the hot and humid climate. His lesser input affects the economic production on the whole. It results either in the forming of deficit areas or of only small surpluses. On the other hand, temperate climates are invigorating as in the European countries. This results in bigger production and large surpluses for trade.

(ii) Natural Vegetation : Because of differences in climate, the natural vegetation is different. For example, tropical regions have forests of hardwood trees. Their uses and importance are different from the forests of temperate regions which have softwood trees. Their uses and the resultant products are different. The direction and the movement of such products is affected.

(iii) Animal life : Climate makes natural animal life different from place to place. Equatorial regions have more reptiles and birds. That is why the equatorial countries have started exporting crocodile and snake skins as fashion commodities for bags, shoes, etc. The other locations do not have these commodities. This results in a regular demand.

(iv) Agriculture : Areas having tropical climate grow rice, jute, rubber, sugarcane, cotton, mango and pineapple, etc. These crops do not grow widely in temperate areas, thus, their demand exists there. Similarly, the temperate regions grow wheat, barley, rye, oats. sugar beet and all types of temperate fruits. Many of the newly invented hybrid and high-yielding varieties of crops flourish only in certain climatic zones. This limitation affects the trade pattern.

(v) Livestock : Certain climatic areas favour the rearing of good breeds of sheep, cows and goats. Such areas do not have the menace of many animal diseases. Denmark, New Zealand and Australia flourish in dairy products, wool and meat while the tropical countries do not rear partly due to unfavourable climate.

(vi) Cost of production : Differences in climate result in some added expenditure or its absence. It affects the overall cost of production. For example, the amount of irrigation required, the type and amount of controls required against pests and diseases of plants, the type of machinery required according to the type of crops grown - all these differ in the different climatic areas. For example, because of a particular climate found in the Prairies, wheat is grown extensively. Wheat production allows the use of machinery at many stages, unlike rice production in which manual labour is required on a large scale. Thus different combinations of factors of climate result in bringing in more differences. Certain products require expensive handling and storage. This, too, affects the overall cost.

(vii) Difference in demands and needs : Further, differences in climate create differences in demand and needs. For example, tropical areas like India would not have a demand for fur or wool but temperate areas have a large demand for them, due to very cold climate. Hence, Australia, Argentina and New Zealand send wool to the Northern temperate lands of the world. But some tropical beverages have a high demand in temperate countries. e.g. tea, cocoa, coffee, etc. U.S.A. and Canada import tea from India and Sri Lanka.

(c) Availability of minerals : Nature has been kind to certain countries regarding mineral wealth, e.g. Brazil, the Russian Federation, Canada, the U. S. A., Iran, Iraq, etc. The minerals are exported by those countries which have a limited demand for these products within their country because of less population pressure or less or no industrialisation. Russian Federation and the U.S.A. use their mineral production because of heavy industrialisation but the minerals from Brazil and the Middle-Eastern countries enter the world trade. The plateau regions and the old mountain blocks are rich in minerals. e.g. the plateau of South Africa. Further, some minerals are very precious, e.g. gold, diamonds, platinum, radium, etc. These minerals enter the World trade.

(II) Human Factors :

- The 'size. distribution and the cultural background of population affects trade :

(a) Size of population : This factor has a far-reaching effect on trade. Some large and densely populated countries have a large internal trade but in the international market they do not play a very important role, e.g. India. Most of their products Are consumed in the home-market. On the other hand, some small-sized population groups, like the cloves production in Zanzibar and Pemba islands, have an excess to be exported on a large scale. The Russian Federation is a large producer of wheat, but not a very important exporter, while Argentina, being a smaller producer than Russian Federation, has managed to be an exporter of wheat just because of its small-sized population. Population size affects the cost of production of commodities. Cheap labour affects the cost of goods of labour-intense industries and competes favourably with the expensive labour of the sparsely populated, countries.

(b) Human skills : Some human groups, because of their cultural background, have the skill which they inherit from their ancestors regarding the making of certain special goods. e.g. Chinese and Japanese inherit the art of special   silk-weaving, painting and crockery making: the handicrafts of Indians, the fashion designing of French people and certain kinds of "carpet weaving of Middle Eastern groups of countries and India. But these articles form luxury goods and are not essential for the economic development of nations.

(III) Industrialisation :

- Industrialisation has greatly stimulated world trade. Industries require a constant flow of raw materials and a market for their manufactured commodities. Hence, if raw material is not available in nearby areas, it is brought from distant lands, e.g. Japan imports iron-ore from India and Australia and goods manufactured in Japan are sold all over the world.

(IV) Political Status and Economic development :

- The political status and the stage of economic development affect trade. For example, in the past, colonial India exported raw material e.g. cotton, manganese, etc. because she had not developed economically. After independence and its resulting industrial development, she uses this raw material and now has started exporting some manufactured goods, e.g. textiles, iron and steel goods, machine tools, etc. In Japan, the traditional exports of tea, silk and handicrafts have given way to manufactured goods. On the whole the total volume and variety of goods traded in the world has expanded because of an overall change in economic development of the world as a whole.

(V) Foreign Capital :

- The amount of foreign investment affects the volume, type and pattern of trade significantly for the developing countries of the world. These countries have a very small capital to invest in new capital intensive industries. The richer nations, e.g. Germany, the U. S. A., Canada, the Russian Federation and France avail of such opportunities and provide the capital and the technical' know-how to these countries. In exchange they obtain the raw materials and other stuffs they need, and also secure a ready market for their industrial goods. Heavy monetary returns and employment for their people are the gains of such rich countries while economic and industrial development are the gains of the developing countries. But such a state of affairs leads to the debtor country following the dictates of the investing countries.

(VI) Means of transportation :

- Wherever good and efficient means of transport are available, trade is encouraged. The navigable Great Lakes of America area favourable factor for much of the trade that takes place there. Similarly, much of the teak moves southwards from Northern Myanmar along the river Irrawaddy. The logs are carried till the mouth of river from where they are exported. The ports of Mumbai and Calcutta in India are very well connected with the rest of India from where goods come for export, or to where the imported goods can be distributed easily. Inland waterways have a favourable influence upon trade especially in South America and Africa where rail-roads are inadequate. Even in otherwise advanced countries, rivers like the Rhine, Rhone, Mississippi, etc. greatly help in the movement of goods.

- In the past trade was restricted to small areas. Its volume was small because of scarce means of transport. Now, with an advancement in science and technology, the transport has developed regarding volume, intensity, frequency and type. More exchanges of kinds of goods can take place even in difficult and remote areas. Earlier the movement of perishable goods was a problem not any more, with the introduction of refrigeration. Well connected canal systems, air-transport, more, and faster vehicles - all have contributed to quick exchanges of things. The opening of the Panama canal gave a boost to world trade by shortening distances. After its opening the trade between the western coastal countries of South America (Peru, Chile) and the eastern coasts of the U.S.A. and European countries developed. The South American countries are rich in minerals like iron-ore, copper and nitrates. These countries export these minerals to the U.S.A. and West European countries through the Panama Canal and import mining machinery, chemicals and manufactured goods from these countries. Even the goods from eastern U. S. A. move through this passage to the western parts of the U. S. A.

(VIII) Government Policy :

- Different countries have different government systems. Government at times, wants to boost some of its economic activities and thus gives protection. These activities flourish and these goods may enter world trade. Tea, jute goods and cotton textile productions are looked after by the Indian government by providing protection through its special export policy. On the other hand, imports of certain goods have to face restrictions at the hands of the government. Government imposes tariffs. It encourages home productions of such goods. Government of India imposes restrictions on the imports of machine parts and oil. Thus, the types of tariffs (taxes or duties levied on imported articles), taxes, licences, subsidies (tax-relief to keep home-prices down), quotas - these are the tools through which government either encourages or discourages trade.

Types of Commodities Traded :

- As a result of the factors mentioned above, the volume of trade and types of goods traded. In the modern world, trade is not limited to commodities which are in short supply locally or commodities which help in raising the level of the standard of living, but it involves the exchange of industrial raw materials, manufactured goods, and many other commodities which are the luxuries of life. The entire picture of trade has become so complex that formal international trade agreements, trade unions, trade groups are part economic activity.

The main commodities entering world trade are mainly as follows :

(1) Industrial raw materials : Agro-based industries require raw materials like raw cotton, jute and rubber and these raw materials enter world trade on a large scale. Egypt and Pakistan export cotton, Bangladesh exports jute, Malaysia exports rubber. The manufacturing industries require minerals on a large scale which are often imported from distant countries, e.g. Japan imports iron-ore from Australia and India, the U. S. A. imports nitrates from Chile.

(ii) Food stuffs : These include grains, beverages, meat, spices, dairy products etc. More countries export food than any other commodity. In such countries, usually one or two crops dominate the structure of exports. Food commodities are exported from the U.S.A., Canada. Australia and Argentina to European and Asian countries. In these exporting countries the size of the population is comparatively small. So, there is always a surplus. On the other hand, the European and the Asian countries have a large population. Wheat from Canada, Australia and Argentina; dairy products and meat from New Zealand and Australia; coffee from Brazil; tea from Sri Lanka and 'India are some of the other items entering world trade.

(iii) Fuels : Coal, petroleum, natural gas, etc. are major power resources. These are mostly imported by the industrially advanced countries of the world. The U. S. A. imports petroleum. India's smaller home production also forces her to import petroleum from the developing countries. Venezuela and the Middle-East countries are the exporters.

(iv) Manufacturers and Machinery : Manufactured goods fall under two categories :

(a) Consumer goods, e.g. textiles, watches, electronic goods.

(b) Producer goods, e.g. steel, machine parts, etc. which form the raw material for further productions.

• The leading nations exporting these commodities are the U. S. A., Germany, the U K, Canada, Belgium, France, etc.

Types of Trade :

Classification of the types of trade is as follows :

(1) Internal or national trade : This type of trade is carried on within a country. It is called retail trade and wholesale trade. The main aim of this exchange is to fulfil the needs of the population in general, e.g. wheat is transported from Punjab and Haryana to the southern states while rice grown in southern states is sold in the northern parts of India. Profits on a large scale are not the sole aim at this level of trade.

(2) International trade : When two or more different countries exchange goods, it is known as international trade. Such trade is mostly done to earn large scale profits. For example, Indian handicrafts, silks, spices, tea are exported to the U. K. while the U. K exports machinery and chemicals to India.

Trade 'involves two things :

Exports : In this type of exchange, the goods are sold out. and go out of a country.

Imports : The goods are bought in from other countries.

Balance of Trade : The comparative volume of imports and exports determines the balance of trade. It can be of three types :

(a) Adverse balance of trade : When the value of imports is more than the value of the exports, it is known as adverse balance of trade.

(b) Favourable balance of trade: On the other hand, when the value of exports is more than that of its imports, it is known as favourable balance of trade.

(c) Balanced trade : Balanced trade is the condition in which the value of exports and imports is more or less the same. This is the state which is desired by most countries.

- **Index of volume of trade :** The volume of international trade is taken as an economic barometer to measure a country's economic well-being. The volume can be measured in terms of weight of goods or value of goods which is a better measure. Sometimes it is measured on a per capita basis, i.e. the value per head of the population of that country.

Advantages of International trade :

Advantages of imports :

(I)　When a country does not possess the essentials for the production of a particular commodity, it can still get them because of the possibility of imports. For example, the Middle East countries can get all the manufactured goods they may want even when they do not have large scale industries of their own. The U. S. A. obtains tea and coffee, which cannot grow in their country, through imports.

(ii)　If the people of a particular country can use their labour, time and energy to produce a better type of commodity, they need not waste their time in producing low-value goods which they can import from other countries. In this way, the economy of labour is achieved. For example, the U.S.A. has preferred investing more labour and capital in the capital- intensive industries and has preferred to import consumer products from Hongkong, Singapore, Korea, Taiwan, etc. This policy has given a big boost to her economy.

(iii)　During natural calamities the imports of essential goods help to reduce the impact of the disaster. Food and other industrial raw materials can be obtained even when those goods are destroyed within the country by unforeseen events like floods, earth-quakes, volcanic eruptions and drought. During certain drought years whenever India falls short of food-grains, she imports wheat, grain from other countries.

Advantages of exports :

(i)　Whenever a country has an abundance of some natural resources, its products can be fully utilized if exports are carried out rather than letting them go waste. For example, Canada has a lot of fertile land with temperate climate which produces an abundance of wheat. This is fully utilized by the countries where the demand for wheat exists.

(ii)　Exports help in specialisation. The possibility of specialisation gives a boost to a more appropriate division of labour and a more productive use of the energy of humanity. Manufacturing of different varieties of electronic goods in Japan was encouraged because it led to exports of this commodity. Different varieties of electronic goods of high quality are made just because of the possibility of exports.

Major Direction of World Trade and Relative Position of Development and Developing countries :

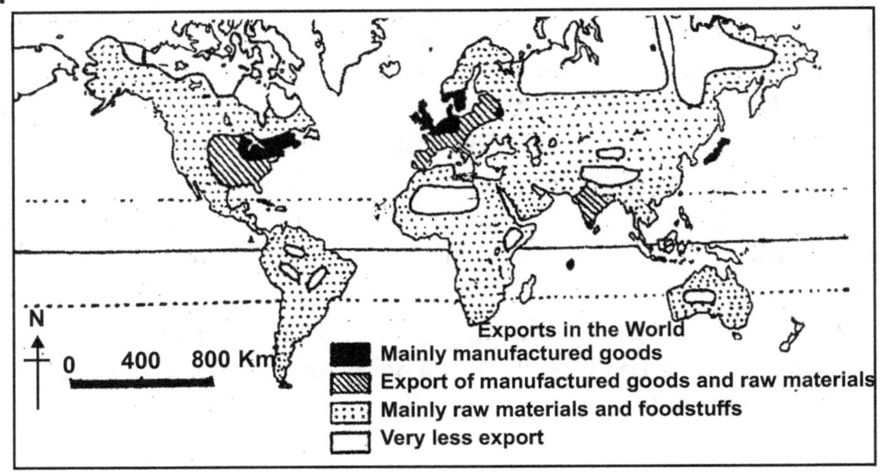

Map. 4.1

Developed Countries :

- The countries which are economically well-off, have a comparatively higher per capita-income, have a sound agricultural base and a stable industrial structure, are called the developed countries. The countries which are trying to attain these aforesaid standards and at present have a lot of scope of development in the field of agriculture and industry, are called the developing countries. The developed countries import raw materials and export manufactured goods because of their advanced stage of industrialisation. The developing countries, on the other hand, mostly export raw materials and import manufactured goods. The pattern and direction of trade of all such countries is as follows :

- **Western Europe :** Western Europe leads the world in the volume of international trade. It has a volume of trade about one-third of that of the world. The U.K., Germany, and France exchange more goods than any other nation except the U. S. A. But, to a large extent, the West European countries trade with one another. The chief international commercial centres are London, Paris, Rotterdam, Antwerp and Hamburg. Its immense volume of trade is due to the following reasons.

(a) High intensity of demands : The needs are more, because of the over-all high density of population and high purchasing power of people. The demands are of two categories : (i) Food and (ii) Industrial raw material.

(b) Large scale industrialisation.

(c) Healthy political relations.

- **The U. S. A. :** The U. S. A. has the second largest volume of trade. Large scale industrialisation has led to a shift from exports of raw materials to that of manufactured goods. There is a very large scale trade between Canada and the U. S. A. and between the two countries on one hand and Europe on the other.

The U. S. A. has the largest volume of trade as one country because of the following factors :

(i)　Richness and variety in natural resources,

(ii)　Large scale industrialisation,

(iii)　An elaborate and extensive system of transport and communication,

(iv)　Liberal Capital,

(v)　Good planning,

(vi)　An inventive bent of mind in the present population.

- Apart from Canada and the West-European countries, her exports go to Venezuela, Japan, Mexico and Australia. Machines, iron and steel, automobiles, air-crafts, wheat, oil-seeds, paper, paper-pulp, fruit and tobacco are the exports. The U. S. A. imports. iron-ore, timber, newsprint and coal from Canada; oil, tin, bauxite, coffee, cocoa, sugar, nuts from Caribbean countries; wool, meat, dairy products from Australia and Argentina; textiles and cars from Japan and Korea.

- **Canada :** Canada exports timber, wood-pulp, paper, wheat, wheat-flour, nickel aluminium, Iron, uranium, vehicles, air-crafts, steel and farm machinery mostly to its neighbour U. S. A. and to the West-European countries.

- **Russian Federation :** The country, because of political reasons, carries out most of its trade with some countries, i.e. East-European countries. It imports rubber from Malaysia, Sugar from Cuba and some light machine parts from India. On the whole it is a self-sufficient country.

- **Australia and New Zealand :** They have a small volume of trade. Most' of their exports are agricultural and pastoral in nature. The export items are wool, meat, dairy products, wheat, sugar, fruit, iron, bauxite, copper, lead, gold, coal, automobiles, rail cars, textiles and chemicals. Their imports are petroleum and machinery.

- **Japan :** It is a highly industrialised nation producing a vast number of manufactured goods. It exports machinery, ships, automobiles, chemicals and a number of electronic goods to the U. S. A. and the European countries. It imports oil from the Middle East countries and the East Indies; cotton, coal and timber from the Asian countries.

Developing Countries :

- **South American Countries :** Most of these countries export tropical food-stuffs and other raw material, and import machinery and-other manufactured goods from North America and Europe.

- **African Countries :** Here, too, the Major exports are mostly raw materials (e.g. rubber, oil, copper) and tropical food-stuffs (banana, cocoa, coffee, nuts).Nigeria exports palm-oil. petroleum; Ghana exports cocoa; East-African countries (Uganda, Kenya, Tanzania, Malawi) export mainly cotton, coffee, hemp, tea and cloves; South Africa exports gold diamonds, antimony and manganese. Import items of Africa are manufactured goods, e.g. machinery, mining equipment and vehicles.

- **China :** It exchanges some food stuffs. Recently, it has also started exporting manufactured goods especially the consumer goods.

- **Middle-Eastern countries like Saudi Arabia :** These countries are important for world trade in oil. They import almost all other things which they need e.g., food-stuffs, manufactured goods, electronic goods, textiles from India, Pakistan, the U. S. A., European countries, Japan, Korea and China.

Some International Organizations Related to Commerce

(1) OPEC : (Organization of Petroleum Exporting Countries) : It is an international commodity organization which seeks to co-ordinate petroleum production and pricing policies in member petroleum exporting countries. The organization was formally established in 1960 following a series of initiatives by Venezuela to encourage co-operative action among petroleum producing countries. Current members, in addition to the founding members of Iran, Iraq, Kuwait, Libya, Saudi Arabia and Venezuela, includes Algeria, Ecuador, Gabon, Indonesia, Nigeria, Qatar and the UAE. The organization's activities have evolved from maintaining export price floors and negotiating petroleum export price and production ceilings and providing financial assistance for developing countries. The supreme authority of the organization is the conference which meets biannually to consider and approve prices and production strategy for members. A long-standing pattern of negotiated uniform price increases was altered in 1976 by the emergence of a dual price structure which formalized internal disagreement regarding pricing policy. Although a single price level was temporarily restored in 1977, the organization's price structure has subsequently tended to reflect the divergent pricing strategies of members, led by Saudi Arabia, who favour price moderation, and members such as Algeria, Iran and Libya who have adopted a more aggressive pricing policy. In addition, the organization provides loans, via the OPEC Special Fund, to finance both balance of payments deficits and development projects in non-OPEC developing countries.

(2) European Economic Community (EEC) : The European Economic Community was established by a separate treaty signed in Rome on 25th March 1957 (and became effective from 1st January 1958) to create a common market and to approximate economic policies.

- **Members :** Its members are Austria, Belgium, Denmark, Finland, France. Germany, Greece, Ireland, Italy, Luxembourg, the Netherlands, Portugal, Spain, Sweden and the United kingdom.

- **Principles :** The aim of community is to establish a common market and to promote throughout the community a harmonious development of economic activities.

- **Activities :** The activities include :

(a) The elimination between member states of customs duties and of quantitative restrictions in regard to the import and export of goods.

(b) The establishment of a common customs tariff and a common commercial policy towards third world countries.

(c) The abolition between member states of the obstacles to the free movement of persons, services and capital.

(d) The inauguration of common agricultural policy.

(e) The establishment of a system ensuring that competition shall not be distorted in the common market.

(f) The inauguration of common transport policy.

(g) The creation of a European social fund in order to improve the possibilities of employment for workers and to contribute to the raising of their standard of living.

(h) The association of overseas countries and territories with community with view to increasing trade and to pursuing jointly their effort toward economic and social development.

(3) The General Agreement on Tariffs and Trade (GATT) : The General Agreement on Tariffs and Trade is not an international organization in a strict sense, but is usually listed among the specialized agencies.

- The GATT is engaged in close consultation with regard to the balance of payments need for imposing restrictions. A significant number of countries have sought membership of GATT.

- The GAIT was created through agreement among trading nations, it did not have the international standing of the International Monetary Fund (IMF) or the World Bank.

- **Achievements :** The great liberalization of tariffs and trade in the post-war period was achieved under the auspices of the GATT.

- The very success of the multilateral tariff negotiations conducted under aegis of the, GATT was so remarkable that the world has became interdependent at an unprecedented rate. As transport costs and tariff barriers have fallen and ease of communication has increased, trade in services is booming, foreign investment is rising sharply.

- The key principle to which the GATT contracting parties subscribed was an open and non-discriminatory trade, thus giving rise to the term "open multinational system".

- GATT contracting parties did not commit to zero tariffs. Under GATT auspices, it was anticipated that they would undertake a series of negotiating rounds in which "trade concessions" would be exchanged.

- Unfortunately the developing countries were not benefiting as much as they might have from the growth of world economy, while the "balance of payments" provisions of the GATT were liberally interpreted to enable developing countries to maintain quantitative restrictions, often including import prohibitions, on their imports. One consequence was that developing countries were losing shares of their world markets.

- Then everything changed suddenly in 1994, the Uruguay Round of trade negotiations under GATT ended with an agreement to found the World Trade Organization which came into being on 1st January 1995.

- The staff of the World Trade Organization (WTO) was the same as that of former GATT and the WTO was housed the same building as the GATT had been and the Deputy General of the GATT became Deputy General of the WTO.

(4) G - 15 : It is an International Organization and was founded in 1990. Its member countries are :

(1) India,	(5) Egypt,	(9) Mexico,	(13) Venezuela,
(2) Algeria,	(6) Indonesia,	(10) Nigeria,	(14) Yugoslavia,
(3) Argentina,	(7) Jamaica,	(11) Peru,	(15) Zimbabwe.
(4) Brazil	(8) Malaysia,	(12) Senegal,	

G-15 is the core group of G-17 and non-aligned nations.

- **Objectives :** To enhance North-South co-operation and consultations on economic issues among them. This platform is proving effective in initiating North-South dialogue on global development problems.

4.1.2 Inter Regional Vs International Trade

- Inter-regional trade refers to trade between regions within a country. Ohlin calls it as inter-local trade. It is the domestic or internal trade.
- International trade is trade between two nations or countries.
- The Classical economists held that there is a fundamental difference between the two types of trade, whereas Modern economists like Bertil Ohlin believed that the difference between the inter-regional and international trade is of "degree" and not of kind.
- The fundamental features in which inter-regional trade differ from international trade are as follows:

(1) Factor immobility : The Classical economists believed that the factors of production are freely mobile within each region with regard to place and occupations and immobile between countries entering into international trade. Thus, labour and capital are regarded as immobile between the countries while they are perfectly mobile within the country.

- The reasons for international immobility of labour are differences in languages, customs, occupational skills, unwillingness to leave familiar surroundings and family ties, the high travelling expenses to the foreign country and restrictions imposed by the foreign country on labour-immigration.
- The international mobility of capital is restricted not by transport costs so much but more by the difficulties of political uncertainty, legal redressal system, ignorance of the prospects of investment in a foreign country, imperfections of the banking system, instability of foreign currencies, mistrust of the foreigners, etc.
- Thus widespread legal and other restrictions exist in mobility of labour and capital between countries. But such problems do not arise in case of inter-regional trade.

(2) Differences in Natural Resources : Different countries tend to specialise in the production of those goods in which they are richly gifted by nature and trade with others where such resources are scarce. For example, in Australia, land is in abundance but labour and capital are relatively scarce. On the other hand, capital is relatively abundant and cheap in England while land is scarce. Thus, commodities requiring more capital such as manufactures can be produced in England; while commodities such as wool, mutton, wheat, etc., requiring more land can be produced in Australia. The two countries can trade each other's commodities on basis of comparative cost differences in the production.

(3) Geographical and Climatic Differences : Every country cannot produce all commodities due to geographical and climatic conditions. For example, Brazil has favourable climate and geographical conditions for the production of coffee; Cuba for beet sugar' Bangladesh for jute etc. Thus countries can specialise in the production of particular commodities and trade them with others.

(4) Different Markets : International markets are separated by differences in language, habits, taste, systems of weights and measures, pattern and styles in machinery, etc. For example, British railway engines and freight cars are basically different from those in France or in U.S.

- Thus, goods which may be traded within regions may not be sold in other countries due to differences in its specifications/features.

- In many cases, products to be sold in foreign countries are specially designed to confirm to the national characteristics of that country.

- Another significant difference between inter-regional and international market is related to the manufacture and sale of goods for regional and international markets.

- A big firm may be producing and selling a number of products in different countries, hence it may not be able to enjoy economies of large-scale production.

- On the other hand, a firm which specialises in the production of only one of product for inter-regional markets may enjoy the economies of large-scale production.

(5) Different Currencies : The principal difference between inter-regional and international trade lies in the use of difference currencies in foreign trade and it is the use of same currency in domestic trade. For example, the currency of India is Rupee which is accepted throughout India. But, if we cross over to Nepal or Pakistan, we must convert Indian rupee into their currency to buy goods and services in those countries.

- It is not differences in currencies alone that are important in international trade, but changes in their relative values.

- Every time a change occurs in the value of one currency in terms of another, a number of economic problems arise.

- Moreover, different countries follow different monetary and foreign exchange policies which influence the supply of exports or demand for imports.

- Thus, difference in policies rather than the existence of different national money which distinguish foreign from domestic trade- Kindleberger.

(6) Problem of Balance Of Payments (BOP) : The problem of BOP is perpetual in international trade while regions within a country have no such problem. This is because there is greater mobility of capital within regions than between countries. The policies which a country chooses to correct its disequilibrium in BOP such as devaluation, over-valuation of currency etc., give rise to further problems. But such problems do not arise in the case of inter-regional trade.

(7) Transport Costs : Due to geographical distances, trade between countries involves high transport costs as against trade between regions within a country.

(8) Different Political Groups : A significant difference between the two types of trade is that all regions within a country belong to one political unit while different countries have different political units.

- Inter-regional trade is among those belonging to the same country. They have a sense of belonging to one country and even the government is interested more in the welfare of its nationals belonging to different regions.

- In international trade there is no cohesion among nations and every country trades with other country in its own interest.

- As remarked by Friedrich List, "Domestic trade is among us, international trade is between us and them".

(9) Different National Policies : The difference between the two trades is in policies relating to commerce, trade, taxation, etc. These policies are same within a country. But, in international trade there are artificial barriers in the form of tariffs, quotas, etc., on the movement of goods and services from one country to another.

- Modern economists find little difference between inter-regional and international trade. Bertil Ohlin mentions that international trade is but a special case of inter-local or inter-regional trade. The reasons why the two trades should be considered similar are as follows:

(1) Ohlin disagrees that labour and capital are freely mobile within a country but immobile internationally. He argues that labour and capital are immobile even within a country. This can be proved from the fact that wage rates differ in different regions within the same country in the same trade. Similarly, interest-rates vary for different purposes in different regions. Further, labour and capital have, in fact, moved between countries, i.e., it is mobile between different nations.

(2) The basis of international trade is not much different from interregional trade. In both the trades goods move from place of abundance to scarcity. Transport costs are involved in both the trades and profit-maximising are the purpose of the two kinds of trade.

(3) Difference in currency does not make it necessary for a separate theory. The currency of one country is convertible into the currency of another country, thus there is no basic difference between international trade and interregional trade.

(4) Ohlin argues that the theory of comparative costs is not applicable to international trade alone but to all trade within a country. It is in fact the principle of specialisation that an individual will devote his abilities to those activities for which he is best suited. For example, the manager of a firm may be able to repair his motor car more cheaply and efficiently than a mechanic at a garage but he does not do so because his time and energy can be more profitably employed in attending to his business.

4.2 IMPORTANCE OF TRANSPORTATION IN COMMERCIAL DEVELOPMENT - SALIENT FEATURES, MERITS AND LIMITATIONS

4.2.1 Transportation

Transportation Features and Modes :

- A key objective of product distribution is to get products into customers' hands in a timely manner. While delivery of digital products can be handled in a fairly smooth way by allowing customers to access their purchase over the internet or mobile app (e.g., download software, gain access to subscription material), tangible products require a more careful analysis of delivery options in order to provide an optimal level of customer service. But as we noted earlier, "optimal" does not always translate into fastest.

- In terms of delivering products to customers, there are six distinct modes of transportation: air, digital, pipeline, rail, truck, and water. However, not all modes are an option for all marketers. Each mode offers advantages and disadvantages on key transportation features that include:

Product Options :

- This feature is concerned with the number of different products that can realistically be shipped using a certain mode. Some modes, such as pipeline, are very limited in the type of products that can be shipped while others, such as a truck, can handle a wide range of products.

Speed of Delivery :

- This refers to how quickly it takes products to move from the shipper's location to the buyer's location.

Accessibility :

- This transportation feature refers to whether the use of a mode can allow final delivery to occur at the buyer's desired location or whether the mode requires delivery to be off-loaded onto other modes before arriving at the buyer's destination. For example, most deliveries made via air must be loaded onto other transportation modes, often trucks, before they can be delivered to the final customer.

Cost :

- The cost of shipment is evaluated in terms of the cost-per-item to cover some distance (e.g., mile, kilometer). Often for large shipments of tangible products cost is measured in terms of tonnes-per-mile or metric-tonnes-per-kilometer.

Capacity :

- Refers to the amount of product that can be shipped at one time within one transportation unit. The higher the capacity the more likely transportation cost can be spread over more individual products leading to lower transportation cost-per-item shipped.

Intermodal Capable :

- Intermodal shipping occurs when two or more modes can be combined in order to gain advantages offered by each mode. For instance, in an intermodal method called piggybacking, truck trailers are loaded onto railroad cars without the need to unload the trailer. When the railroad car has reached a certain destination the truck trailers are off-loaded onto trucks for delivery to the customer's location.

Advantages and Disadvantages of transport

Advantages:

1. **Less Capital Outlay :**
- Road transport required much less capital Investment as compared to other modes of transport such as railways and air transport. The cost of constructing, operating and maintaining roads is cheaper than that of the railways. Roads are generally constructed by the government and local authorities and only a small revenue is charged for the use of roads.

2. **Door to Door Service :**
- The outstanding advantage of road transport is that it provides door to door or warehouse to warehouse service. This reduces cartage, loading and unloading expenses.

3. **Service in Rural Areas :**
- Road transport is most suited for carrying goods and people to and from rural areas which are not served by rail, water or air transport. Exchange of goods, between large towns and small villages is made possible only through road transport.

4. **Flexible Service :**
- Road transport has a great advantage over other modes of transport for its flexible service, its routes and timings can be adjusted and changed to individual requirements without much inconvenience.

5. **Suitable for Short Distance :**
- It is more economic and quicker for carrying goods and people over short distances. Delays in transit of goods on account of intermediate loading and handling are avoided. Goods can be loaded directly into a road vehicle and transported straight to their place of destination.

6. **Lesser Risk of Damage in Transit :**
- As the intermediate loading and handling is avoided, there is lesser risk of damage, breakage etc. of the goods in transit. Thus, road transport is most suited for transporting delicate goods like chinaware and glassware, which are likely to be damaged in the process of loading and unloading.

7. Saving in Packing Cost :

- As compared to other modes of transport, the process of packing in motor transport is less complicated. Goods transported by motor transport require less packing or no packing in several cases.

8. Rapid Speed :

- If the goods are to be sent immediately or quickly, motor transport is more suited than the railways or water transport. Water transport is very slow. Also much time is wasted in booking the goods and taking delivery of the goods in case of railway and water transport.

9. Less Cost :

- Road transport not only requires less initial capital investment, the cost of operation and maintenance is also comparatively less. Even if the rate charged by motor transport is a little higher than that by the railways, the actual effective cost of transporting goods by motor transport is less. The actual cost is less because the motor transport saves in packing costs and the expenses of intermediate loading, unloading and handling charges.

10. Private Owned Vehicles :

- Another advantage of road transport is that big businessmen can afford to have their own motor vehicles and initiate their own road services to market their products without causing any delay.

11. Feeder to other Modes of Transport :

- The movement of goods begins and ultimately ends by making use of roads. Road and motor transport act as a feeder to the other modes of transport such as railways, ships and airways.

Disadvantages :

- Inspite of various merits, road/motor has some serious limitations:

1. Seasonal Nature :

- Motor transport is not as reliable as rail transport. During rainy or flood season, roads become unfit and unsafe for use.

2. Accidents and Breakdowns :

- There are more chances of accidents and breakdowns in case of motor transport. Thus, motor transport is not as safe as rail transport.

3. Unsuitable for Long Distance and Bulky Traffic :

- This mode of transport is unsuitable and costly for transporting cheap and bulky goods over long distances.

4. Slow Speed :

- The speed of motor transport is comparatively slow and limited.

5. Lack of Organisation :

  The road transport is comparatively less organised. More often, it is irregular and undependable. The rates charged for transportation are also unstable and unequal.

- The desirable features of mass transit systems are balanced by a number of serious drawbacks. In the first place, such systems are economically feasible only in areas that have relatively large populations. As the number of inhabitants per square mile decreases, the efficiency of a mass transportation system also decreases.

- Mass transit systems are also very expensive to build and to operate. This factor becomes more important when cities decide to install mass transit systems long after development has already taken place and disruption of existing structures is a serious problem. Since mass transit systems seldom receive the government assistance provided to highway construction, consumers often have to pay a higher fraction of the costs of using mass transportation.

- People complain about mass transportation systems also because they can be crowded, uncomfortable, dirty, and unreliable. Again, with limited budgets, mass transit systems are seldom able to maintain equipment and schedules to the extent that riders can rightly demand.

- Finally, mass transportation systems are simply not as convenient as the automobile. A person can step into her or his car and drive virtually anywhere with a minimum of inconvenience. No mass transportation system can approach this level of ease.

4.2.2 Role of Transportation in Commercial Development

Role of Transportation in Commercial Development :

- Roads, railways, waterways and airways are the major modes of transportation. It is a fact that the development of transportation facilities and the economic development of goes region hand in hand. Hence, economically prosperous areas like eastern U.S.A. and western Europe have well developed transport networks while, on the other hand, backward areas like the Amazon lowlands and the interior parts of large continents like Asia have inadequate transportation network.

- Transportation facilities affect the commercial activities and thus the commercial development of a region in the following ways :

(a) **Agriculture :** Transportation facilities open up new lands and remote regions, if they continue to be remote and inaccessible, may not have be been developed. Large areas can be brought under agriculture and agricultural produce can be sent to the national and international markets only if there are adequate transportation facilities. Large scale commercial farming has been made possible only because of speedy and efficient transport. For instance, only after the vast Prairie lands were linked by trans-continental railways to the eastern coastal areas, could the vast rolling grasslands of North America be brought under agriculture. Now the Prairie region produces wheat on a large scale which is sold in the world market. Refrigeration facilities in transport were responsible for the development of dairy farming in Australia and New Zealand, through which perishable commodities like milk and milk products could be sent to Western Europe. Flowers grown in the Netherlands are sent all over Europe by air. Crops like rubber, tea, coffee and many others grown in the plantations of South and South East Asia are sold all over the world.

Thus, transportation facilities are responsible for development of agriculture in two ways :

   (i)   They help to bring more land under cultivation.

   (ii) They help to carry agricultural produce to the markets.

(2) Mining : Minerals are bulky and heavy, however, the demand for minerals has increased very rapidly since the Industrial Revolution. All industries, directly or indirectly, depend on minerals but, without efficient and cheap means of transportation, it would be difficult to carry minerals to the factories. The railways and waterways have made it possible to transport minerals to the consuming centres. In the initial stages of industrialisation, iron and steel plants were set up in areas where coal and iron-ore were found in close proximity. However, due to continuous exploitation, the local mines were unable to meet the increasing demand. Hence, now-a-days, the minerals are carried to distant areas to the manufacturing plants. Large ocean going vessels, the river boats trucks as well as railways deliver huge quantities of minerals to the manufacturing plants. Take the example of the Western South American countries. The Panama Canal Route has provided the shortest route between these countries and the eastern U.S.A. and West European countries. Today iron-ore, copper and nitrates are mined on a large scale in South American countries and these minerals are sent to the Eastern U.S.A. and Western Europe. The economy of these countries has prospered because of mining, which depends on efficient and cheap water transport. Many iron and coal mines were opened up in Siberia due to the opening up of the Trans Siberian Railway. Thus the mining activity assumed unprecedented importance after industrialisation and this credit goes largely to modern means of transportation.

(3) Fishing and rearing of animals : Now-a-days, large fishing vessels have made it possible to carry out fishing on a commercial basis. These vessels can fish in the waters and are complete with refrigeration plants, canneries and processing facilities. Thus fishing started on a very large scale, with the introduction of such modern fishing vessels Refrigeration facilities are also available in land transport, by which fish can be carried to long distances from the coast. This large scale fishing has helped to strengthen the economies of many countries in the temperate lands, e.g. Japan, China, U.S.A., Chile, Peru and Norway. Many of these countries export fish.

- The economies of many semi-arid areas of the world depend on the rearing of animals, e.g. Australia and Argentina. These areas produce animal products like meat, milk and milk products which are highly perishable. Modern transportation facilities have made it possible to rear the animals on a large scale. Aeroplanes and ships with refrigeration facilities carry these products to the western markets. Although Australia, New Zealand and Argentina are far away from the major markets, they have prosperous economies that are partly based on rearing of animals and the credit goes to the modern transportation facilities.

(4) Manufacturing : Today, the prosperity of many highly developed countries like the U.S.A. Japan, the U. K. Germany and many other West European countries is largely due to manufacturing. This economic activity depends on the arteries of transportation, as power resources, raw material and labour should assimilate at the manufacturing plants. Many a times the raw material is brought from distant areas. Similarly, the manufactured products are often sent to distant markets. Thus, manufacturing relies heavily on transportation facilities. Japan is a classic example. Its economy has prospered only because of its manufacturing industries. This country is very poor in natural resources. Its ships bring raw material from distant areas and distribute the country's manufactured goods in the world market. Japan's economy depends mainly on the foreign market and without its efficient means of transport, its economy could not have prospered.

- Mumbai is an important cotton textile centre of India. It is well linked by railways to the cotton growing areas of the Deccan plateau as well as to the markets in India.' Similarly. credit should be given to local trains for helping to make it a major industrial city. Thousands of workers live in suburban areas and commute daily through the local trains to the from their work.

(5) Trade : In the past, trade was carried out mainly between neighbouring regions or countries because transport facilities were poor and undeveloped. Trade consisted only of valued articles, such as silk and spices. With the development of railways, ocean and air transport and with the introduction of specialized carriers, like oil tankers and refrigerated ships for perishable commodities, world trade began on a very large scale. The transportation of minerals, forest products, agricultural products, manufactured goods, all form part of world trade and help to develop the economies of the related countries. Oil trade has brought prosperity to the Middle East countries while the prosperous economy of Japan largely depends on import of raw material and export of manufactured goods.

(6) Tourism : Tourism is an important commercial activity. There are several factors that are responsible for its growth. Out of which transportation facilities play an important role. Actually, tourism is the outcome of travel. The provision of adequate, safe, comfortable, fast, convenient and cheap public transport is an essential thing for mass tourism. Air travel, in particular, over the past 20 years has made distant destinations accessible. Previously such tourism was not imaginable. Air transport offers the fastest links over long distances, and the number of tourists visiting different countries has increased on a large scale. Railways are able to carry tourists in large number over long distances. Moreover, they provide the cheapest mode of transport. The beach and hill resorts, places of tourist interests have become accessible due to adequate transportation facilities.

- Tourism has created large scale employment facilities to people in various spheres right from travel agents to guides and from people working in hotels to those who are engaged in developing and maintaining infrastructure.

- Thus, transportation plays an important role in the commercial development of a region or a country.

TYPES OF MODES OF TRANSPORTATION - ROADWAYS, RAILWAYS, AIRWAYS, SEAWAYS AND TYPES OF TRADE ROUTES - SILK ROUTE, CPCC ETC.

4.3.1 Types of mode of transportation-Roadways, Railways, Airways, Seaways

Main Types of Transportation :

Major types of transport are -

(a) Land transport,

(b) Water transport,

(c) Air transport.

Land Transport

(I) Roads :

- Roads have been built since the beginning of historical times. The need for good roads was really felt after the industrial revolution. The introduction of the automobile in the field of transport necessitated surfaced all-weather roads. Today's modern roads have deep foundations of stones which are covered with concrete or asphalt. These tarred roads remain in a good state for several years and promote high speed transportation due to their smooth surfaces.

- Roads are commonly divided into two types, metalled roads and unmetalled roads, of which matalled roads are more important. The metalled roads are further classified into state roads, highways and national highways. In order to facilitate the quick movement of passengers and goods over a long distance, special roads have been built in developed countries of the world. They are known as 'autobahns' in Italy and 'motorways' in Britain. These wide roads run straight over long distances.

Advantages of roads :

(1) Roads can be built on slopes up to 30% gradient and thus can be mountainous areas. This has led to the development of many hill stations. Roads have thus opened up remote areas and have promoted tourism. A large number of hill-stations like Nainital, Mount Abu are accessible only by roads.

(2) Roads can be used by a wide range of modes of transport, namely animals, animal drawn vehicles and many types of automobiles.

(3) Road transport is quicker, more convenient and more flexible than railways. It is particularly convenient for passengers as well as movement of goods over short distances. Door to door collection and delivery is possible in road transport.

(4) As compared to railways, construction of roads is cheap. In developing countries like India, railways mainly connect towns. Roads play an important role in these countries by connecting a large number of villages.

(5) Roads are important to farmers. Good roads help the farmers to move their agricultural produce, especially the perishable products like vegetable, fruits and dairy products to the towns. That is why tuck farming has developed in the vicinity of the cities.

Disadvantage of roads

(1) The large number of vehicles on roads creates traffic jams and congestion in towns.

(2) Due to high speed of vehicles, many accidents take place on roads.

(3) Road transport is costly for long distances.

(II) Railways :

- The railway is also a product of Industrial Revolution. Steam provided power not only to run the machines but also to run the railways. The fast growing industries required materials from different areas as well as markets for their manufactured products. Thus railways are introduced mainly to carry freight over long distances at a cheaper rate.

Advantages of railways :

(1) Railways have proved to be cheapest and the fastest carriers of bulky goods over long distances.

(2) Railways are able to carry large bulks of freight as compared to road vehicles.

(3) Railway construction and expansion has helped in setting up industries, e.g. the cotton textile industry in Mumbai owe their existence and development to the expansion of railways.

(4) In large countries like China and India, quick movement of the army and police from one part of the country to another is necessary in times of external aggression or internal disturbances. Railways are useful for the defence and the able administration of countries.

(5) In many countries, railways are important for carrying passengers. Railways are important in carrying thousands of commuters to the cities.

(6) Underground railways play an important role in large cities like London, Tokyo Moscow. They occupy very little valuable surface in the urban areas, carry thousands of passengers and do not create traffic jams.

(7) Railways are especially important in areas where density of population is high and the standard of living of the people is low'. In such regions few people own cars and cannot afford the costly air-transport. Thus railways are very important in such countries like Pakistan and India.

(8) Railways have also served to open up new lands, e.g. the large temperate grasslands of the Prairies in North America were brought under cultivation when these area were linked by-railways to the eastern coastal areas.

Disadvantages, of railways :

(1) Railways require a relatively levelled ground and cannot negotiate gradients of over 1 in 50. Thus, construction of railways involves several stages like cutting, embankments, bridges, tunnels that serve to keep the gradients low. Thus construction of railway is very costly. Due to this reason very few railways are built in the mountainous area and on deeply dissected plateaus. Plain, level areas with their gentle gradients facilitate the construction of railways.

(2) Trains cannot run without rails and this reduces their flexibility. Unlike roads, they are unable to give door to door service.

(3) The maintenance cost of railways is very high.

(4) If the tracks in one region are of different gauges, then the goods and passengers change trains which causes delays and higher running cost.

(5) Unlike roads, railways do not link small villages with each other.

(6) It is uneconomical to construct railways in sparsely populated areas.

(III) Pipelines :

- Pipelines are traditionally used for carrying a liquid or gas from a point of supply to a point of consumption. They are of variable diameter and length and many-a-times hundreds of Kilometers long. Pipelines may be laid over-ground or underground and even water. Traditionally, they are used to carry liquid or gas, but nowadays they are associated with the petroleum and petroleum industries. Today roughly half a million kilometers of oil pipeline exist in the world.

- Pipelines are expensive to construct and maintain, hence it is necessary to use them to their maximum capacity. The main advantage of pipeline is that they provide a relatively cheap mode of transport for liquid commodities. They can be laid on the sea-bed from off shore wells and linked to on-shore refineries or pipes.

- Majority of the pipelines in the world are owned by specific oil companies.

(IV) Water Transport :

Rivers, canals, lakes, seas and oceans provide waterways for transport. Water trasport play an important role in world transport due to the following reasons :

(1) Water transport does not need tracks like roads or railways and it uses the existing routes like oceans, seas and rivers. It is the cheapest form of transport as no heavy investment is required in laying down tracks or on their maintenance.

(2) Large ocean going vessels can carry high quantities of heavy goods. Modern super oil-tankers carry volumes of oil. These modern ocean vessels reduce transportation costs and hence are extremely useful for carrying cheap and bulky commodities like timber, minerals, etc.

- Today, water transport is indispensable in international trade, especially for carrying raw material and bulky, heavy manufactured goods over long distances. The large open oceans are continuous water-bodies and many of the seas like the Mediterranean and the Red Sea are linked to them, thus providing unbroken water routes. The majority of the large rivers ultimately join the oceans and thus water-bodies extend inland through such rivers and their canals.

There are two types of water transport :
    (i)   Inland water transport.
    (ii) Ocean transport.

(V) Air Transport :
- Air transport is a product of 20th century. It is the fastest mode of transport and has brought together the distant parts of the world. The importance of air transport can be brought out through the following facts :

(1) The effect of relief features is little felt on air transport. It is difficult to construct roads and railways in mountainous areas, forests, deserts and the snow covered areas, hence, air transport proves immensely beneficial in these areas. Small aeroplanes can fly through mountainous regions and they require little space for landing.

(2) Air transport is the fastest means of transport. Many aeroplanes can travel at speed of 800 k.m. per hour. The distance between New York and London is covered within 7.30 hours. Thus, airways save time.

(3) Due to speedy transport, airways are important in the transport of small. light and costly commodities like jewellery, watches, calculators, medicines, light and delicate machinery, mail, etc. These costly goods can bear the high cost of air transportation.

(4) Airways are extremely useful in carrying perishable commodities like flowers, fruits, vegetables, dairy products, meat and fish.

(5) Airways are important during wars in carrying armaments, aid and people. At the time of natural calamities like earthquakes, volcanoes and floods, aeroplanes are used to provide medicines and food packets to the victims.

(6) Air transport is specially important in those countries that are made up of several islands like Japan, the Philippines and Indonesia.

Like other means of transport, air transport is also not without certain drawbacks :

(1) Though air transport is not much hampered by relief features on the earth, it is largely influenced by the atmospheric conditions. Strong winds, heavy rainfall or snowfall, storms, dense fog, all prove dangerous to aviation.

(2) Though aeroplanes can operate in mountainous areas, runways require level land.

(3) As compared to ships and railway aeroplanes have a limited carrying capacity.

(4) Air transport is very costly, hence only people having a high standard of living and high per capita income can travel by air.

(5) Due to high cost of transportation, bulky and cheap commodities like minerals and timber cannot be sent through this mode of transport.

(6) Each country lays claims to its air space and without the prior permission of the respective governments, aeroplanes cannot fly over other territories.

(7) Aerodromes lie away from cities and towns and passengers have to spend valuable time in going to and returning from the air ports.

Use of Carrying Passenger and Freight
Roads :

- Roads are important routes for both passengers and freight transport for small and medium distance. Passenger transport is undertaken both by the public and private sectors. Buses which carry a large number of people are cheaper but they have fixed stops.

- Taxis are usually vary costly. In developed countries like the U. S. A., Canada, Japan and many European countries the percentage of privately owned cars has increased recently. There is one car per 2 persons in these countries. Private cars provide a fairly cheap, extremely convenient way of travel for work or pleasure. For the last 15 years road transport in these countries have become increasingly important for even long distance travel due to the construction of motorways. Hence trains are fast losing their importance in carrying passengers.

- But the picture is different in developing countries like India. Road transport is not much developed and the number of privately owned cars is small.

- The vehicles that run on roads are constantly increasing in size but still they have a limited carrying capacity. Road transport is most economical over relatively short distances and it is becoming important. They are able to give door to door service. Many a time road transport is quicker than railways. Today trucks and vans have been manufactured for special purposes, e.g. tankers for carrying liquid commodities like oil and milk; refrigerated vehicles for carrying perishable products like vegetables, meat and fruits.

- The importance of roads in developed countries of the world has led to a number of social consequences. People in these countries live in distant suburbs and make longer journeys for work, shopping and leisure. Truck farming is the result of modern roadways. This type of agriculture is recently introduced into the agricultural economy because of the modern, efficient trucks which have refrigeration facilities. Truck farming areas lie at a distance of an over-night journey covered by, the trucks by which fresh vegetable, fruits, eggs, meat and flowers are sent to urban markets.

Railways :

- Railways are useful for carrying passengers and freight. Railways are by far the most efficient form of transport for commuters, who live in suburbs and come into the large city every day for work. At a time thousands of commuters can be carried to the cities. In Mumbai the local trains every day carry thousands of commuters to the city and back to their homes in the suburbs. These suburban railways do not create traffic jams.

- Underground railways are ideal for transport in cities like London, Liverpool, Parts and Tokyo. These railways use very little valuable urban space and can carry large number of people from one place to another place according to regular time tables. Thus commuter trains are very important in countries like the U K., the U. S. A. and Japan to carry passengers on a large scale.

- Railways are specially important in countries where the density of population is high and the living standard of the people is low. In such countries like India and China, few people own cars and cannot afford the costly air transport.
- In the developed countries of the world like the West European countries and the U.S.A. the importance of railways for carrying passengers is fast declining. Many people own cars and with their high standard of living they prefer to travel by air rather than by railway. Hence in these countries railways are mainly used for carrying freight.
- Railways can carry loads up to 10,000 tonnes at a fair speed and they are the cheapest and fastest carriers of bulky goods over long distances. They are important for carrying, coal and other minerals, timber etc. Roads are useful to carry freight over small distance while railways are useful over longer distances.

Waterways :

- Waterways provide the cheapest mode of transport. The continents of North and South America and Australia were discovered only a few centuries ago only with the help of water transport. Large scale migration took place from the Old World to New World by the waterways. Today all over the world, the importance of waterways has declined in carrying passengers because such a journey is very slow.
- But waterways play a very important role in carrying cheap and bulky commodities at a cheaper rate. Today greater specialisation of commercial vessels has made freight transportation indispensable through water ways. e.g. Cargo liners combine the function of cargo and passenger transport. They carry commodities such as grain, meat, dairy produce, fruit and wool together with a limited number of passengers. Of all bulk-carriers, the mammoth oil tankers are very important, a number of which now exceed 5,00,000 tonnes dead-weight each.

Airways :

- For long distance travel, aircrafts are extremely useful for passenger transport. In the development countries of the world the standard of living is very high and people can travel by air as air transport is an expensive form of transport.
- In developing countries of the world, very few people travel by air due to a low per capita income.
- Lack of space in aeroplanes restricts the number of persons they can carry. Air transport is costly and is used only for carrying light and valuable goods, e.g. watches, calculators jewellery and mail
- Airways are extremely useful in carrying perishable commodities like flowers, fruits, vegetables, dairy products, meat and fish, e.g. vegetable and fruits grown in California are carried the densely populated eastern areas of the U.S.A by air.

Influence on industries and trade :

- The carrying capacity of road transport is comparatively small as compared to the railways. But still roadways are important in carrying raw materials and semi-finished products to the manufacturing industries and the final products to the market over small distance. Thus, they are responsible for the development and growth of industries and trade.

- Roads also serve an important purpose of opening up areas that are not easily reached by railways. Roads can be built even in mountainous areas. A large number of hill - stations like Mahabaleshwar, Nainital, Manali and Mount Abu are accessible only by roads. Roads also promote tourism, an invisible trade.

- The growth of industries is largely dependent on railways. Many of the manufacturing industries require raw materials in huge quantities and several of them are bulky and cheap in value, e.g. timber, iron-ore, coal etc. These raw materials are obtained from nearby or distance areas. The railways provide an ideal mode of transport for carrying these goods, as well as the workers who work in the factories. At the same time, the finished products can be also sent by railways. Hence railways have a profound impact on the location and development of industries. All the major industrial regions of the world have a dense network of railways.

- Railways have opened up several mining areas of Asiatic Russian Federation. The Trans-Siberian Railway carries these minerals to the highly industrialised Europe region of the country.

- Railways have also served to open up new lands, e.g. the large temperate grass lands of the Prairies in North America were brought under cultivation when these areas were linked by transcontinental railways to, the eastern coastal areas. Today this region exports wheat on a large scale.

Water Ways :

- Ocean routes also have a large influence on the location and growth of industries. Specialised industrial carriers like oil tankers, colliers (for shipping coal), fishing vessels dump raw material at the ports. Instead of carrying these raw materials in the interior areas, the industries are usually set up in the port cities in order to save the inland cost of transportation. That is why the majority of the ports of world are major industrial cities where raw material is assembled from different destinations, e.g. Shanghai, Osaka, Yokohama, London, Mumbai.

- Waterways have greatly accelerated the trade of cheap, bulky commodities, e.g. minerals, timber, wool, grain etc. Fishing vessels have promoted the activity of commercial fishing.

- Airways do not have an impact on the development. of industries or trade. On the other hand, airways are a product of these economic activities. The highly industrialised and commercialised areas are associated with a dense net work of airways. They have promoted international tourism.

Social Factors Associated with Various Modes of Transportation :

Roadways :

(1) Private cars have allowed commuters a much wider range of choice in their place of residence in relation to their place of work. This has resulted in extensive migration from urban areas to rural places.

(2) A large number of cars on the roads creates problems of congestion and traffic jams, especially at peak hours.

(3) Automobiles pour out large amounts of pollutants and are responsible for air pollution.

(4) Noise pollution has become a serious problem in major cities.

(5) Road accidents are considerable.

Railways :

(1) Railways do not create problem of congestion and traffic jams.

(2) The railways that use coal and diesel oil, give out a lot of soot, ash, smoke an various gases and are responsible for air pollution.

(3) People living near railway junctions and stations suffer from noise pollution.

Waterways :

(1) Water ways were mainly responsible for bringing together the peoples of different races, religion and culture. They were responsible for populating the newly discovered continents.

Airways :

(1) The entire world has become smaller due to airways.

(2) Though airways are the fastest mode of transport, aerodromes usually lie away from the centres of cities and towns and passengers have to spend valuable time in going to and returning from the airports.

(3) Air crafts are responsible for noise pollution near airports.

World Distribution of Roads, Railways, Waterways and Airways:

(I) Roads :

Construction of roads is comparatively cheaper then railways but roads have not developed evenly in all parts of the world. Roads are not developed in areas of inhospitable climate as such areas which are sparsely populated and do not provide adequate passengers and goods to cover costs. These areas include the vast ;deserts like the Sahara and the Australian desert: the equatorial and the coniferous forests; the mountainous regions of the world and the Tundras. Further, roads are still not developed in many parts of the developing countries.

Europe : France, Denmark, Italy and Germany and other West European Countries have a dense network of roads. This extends out towards the east and the north. In these regions road transport is of greater significance than the railways. Most of the roads are fine, double-laned, direct, straight roads. These broad, multiple-lane highways can carry heavy and high-speed traffic. Such highways are known as autobahns in Germany, auto routes in France, autostrade in Italy and motorways in the U. K.

North America : Road transport is very important in North America. In the U.S.A. each family has more than one car and in Canada there is one car for every three people. The railways have suffered greatly from the competition of road transport. Beside numerous state highways, the U.S.A. has several trans-continental highways which cover a distance of more then 7500 km. The network of roads is dense in the southern part of Canada where density of population is high. Similarly density of highways is more in the part of the U.S.A. that lies to the east of the river Mississippi. This is highly commercialised, industrialised and densely populated region of the U.S.A.

South America : South America is very poorly served by roads. There are vast equatorial forests, large mountainous areas the vast Pampas where there is a scarcity of stones for surfacing . Moreover, many of the countries are economically backward and the density of population is low. The majority of the roads are unsurfaced. Major highways link major cities of the countries, e.g. a highway linking Caracas, the capital of Venezuela, to the Caribbean port of La Guaria. Many of the countries are trying to develop and improve their roads. The Pan-American Highway links North and South America. It runs from Alaska to Argentina. This highway is 32,000 km in length. This gigantic highway will help to break the economic isolation of many Latin American countries.

Africa : Like South America, the African continent is also very poorly served by roads. A large part of northern Africa is occupied by the Sahara desert. The central part is covered by Equatorial forest, while its eastern part is a highland region. A majority of the countries of Africa are economically backward and sparsely populated. Hence, roads are few. The development of roads is slow and very few roads are surfaced. Nigeria is the most populous and developed country of Africa. It has greatly improved its roads. A major highway links Lagos and Ibadan. Kenya, Tanzania and Zambia have been recently linked by the Great North Road, which links major cities like Lusaka, Nairobi, Mombasa and Dar-es-Salaam, Trans-African Highway project is under consideration, which will link Kenya, Uganda, Zaire, Cameroon and Nigeria. It will help in economic development of these countries.

Australia : The highways in Australia are found in the neighbourhood of ports and linking all the state capitals, e.g. Stuart Highway, Princes Highway. With the growth in number of motor vehicles, road development in Australia is rapid. In the north-eastern part of Australia there are special roacLs, used mainly for transporting cattle. They known as 'beef roads".

• Railways are more important in the Russian Federation country than roads. There are several reasons for the poor development of roads. Firstly, the country is very large long-distance metalled road-building is thus very costly. The northerly regions are covered by snow for a large part of the year, and in the Taiga region, there are extensive forests and marshy areas. The southern part of the country is largely mountainous. Government encourages only the expansion of railways. Thus, compared with the total size of country the length of roads is very little. Even the distribution of roads is very uneven. Comparatively, this network is thick in the European part and extremely thin in the Asiatic part. Moscow is the focus of the roads, from where all roads radiate in different directions towards Leningrad, Gorky, Kazan, Rostov and several other towns.

South and Eastern Asia : Excluding Japan, the majority of the Asian countries have a developing economy and hence roads have been developed only in small areas of this region. As compared to its size, Japan has a great length of highways. In India road transport has more advantages over railways and since 1950, the kilometerage of roads is increasing. Despite the scarcity of funds, the overall development of the road network in India is quite satisfactory. According to the 7th Five Year Plan Report, the country has 20,37,000 km. roadways out of which 10,36,000 kms are unsurfaced and 1001,000 kms. are surfaced roads. These roads are divided into 5 administrative classes, national highways. state highways, major district roads, district roads and village, roads. In Pakistan road construction is in progress but some areas are still poorly served by roads. South East Asian Countries are poorly served by roads. Under the communist regime. CHINA has made large progress in the construction of roads. Today China has more then 6,00,000 kms of roads which are motorable.

(II) Railways :
- Like roads, railways have not developed evenly in all parts of the world. The tundra regions, the equatorial forests, the deserts, the interior parts of the vast continents like Asia have but few railways as these areas are very sparsely populated and are associated with inhospitable climate.

Europe : A dense network of railways is found in the western regions of Europe which gradually thins out towards. the east. This Western region is the highly industrialised and commercially important region of Europe in which movement of raw materials, manufactured goods and passengers is carried out on a large scale. Belgium has the highest density of railways (1 km of railway for every 6.5 sq. km)- Underground railways are also important in many capital cities like London, Paris and Moscow.

North America : Today nearly 40% of the railways are found in North America. Railways are used mostly to carry bulky freight over long distances. The densest railway network is found to the east of 100° West Longitude up to the Atlantic coast and comprises the regions of the Mississippi basin and the eastern region and in Southern Canada. Several trans-continental railways run in the east-west direction linking eastern and western coastal areas of North America.

- The two trans-continental railways of Canada are the Canadian National and the Canadian Pacific railways. These railways run from Montreal and Queebc on the east to Prince Rupart and Vancouver to the west. These railway lines are 5600 km long and carry forest products, minerals and wheat from the western regions to the eastern regions of Canada.
- The Great Northern. the North Pacific, the Union Pacific, the Santa Fe. the Southern Pacific railway are the trans-continental railways of the U. S. A. They are also used to carry bulky commodities between the western region and the eastern region of the country.

America : Railways are developed on a small scale in South America as compared to Europe and North America. The railways are developed mainly in Argentina and South-east Brazil. The trans-continental railway of South America runs from Buenos Aires to Santiago and Valparaiso and joins Argentina and Chile. It. is 1450 km. long and is known the Trans-Andean route. The remaining countries are very poorly served by railways.

Africa : This second largest continent has only 40,000 km of railways. South Africa has the densest network railways due to large scale mining of gold, diamonds and copper. The majority of railways join the coastal ports to the inland cities. The Benguela railway and the Tanzara railway link the Katanga-Zambia copper belt to the coastal areas.

Australia : The distribution of railways is very uneven' in this country also. The large desert of Australia is very poorly served by railways while the largest concentration of railways is found is New South Wales. One trans-continental railway runs from Adelaide in Australia to Perth, which lies at a distance, of 5000 km. to the East of It.

Russian Federation : The European-part of the Soviet Union is well-served by railways. Moscow is the major junction from where railways radiate in different directions. Siberia or the region that lies to the east of the Urals has very few railways as this region is economically backward and sparsely populated. This part is linked to the western part of the country by a trans-continental railway, the Trans-Siberian Railway.

Trans-Siberian Railway :

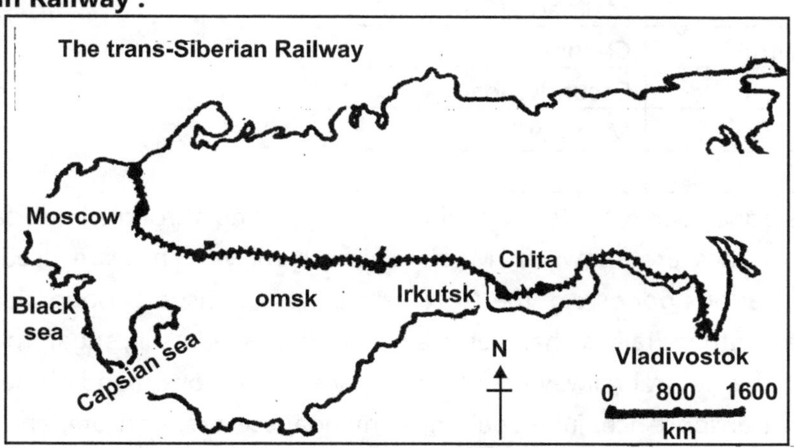

Map 4.2-: Russian Federation

- This is the most important railway line in the Russian Federation. It is 8960 km long and connects Leningrad and Moscow in the West to Vladivostok in the east. This railway joins the sparsely populated Siberian region to the European part of the country. Siberia has large forests and rich deposits of a variety of minerals -which find an outlet in densely populated and highly industrialised European part of the country. This railway has helped in opening up mines in Siberia. Many industries and settlements have developed near the mining areas. This double tracked railway is hardly used for passenger, traffic but is used mainly to carry raw materials from the Asiatic part to the European part of Russian Federation.

South and South East Asia : Japanese railways are famous for their speed and efficiency. The majority of the railways are found in its coastal areas and they are electrified. China's railway network is mainly found in its eastern part. Main trunk routes run from Beijing to Manchuria, Canton and Mongolia. Apart from these three countries, railways have developed only on small scale in other south-east Asian countries.

Railways in India :

Railways play a vital role in the transport of freight and passengers. In 1853 the first railway line was laid between Mumbai and Thane by the British for a distance of 34 km. Today the growth is phenomenal.

- The network is divided into 9 zones and further subdivided into divisions. The 9 zones are :

Table 4.1

Railways	Headquarters
Central	Mumbat
Eastern	Calcutta
North Eastern	New Delhi
North East Frontier	Gorakhpur
Southern	Maligaon (Guwahati)
South Central	Chennai
South Eastern	Secunderabad
Western	Mumbai
Total	

- The various zones serve the surrounding states running through important cities and towns. The main lines are shown in Map 4.3. These railway lines are used to transport passengers and various goods e.g. the Northern railways transport foodgrains, sugar, coal, and timber. The Southern railway handles grain, cotton, oilseeds, salt, sugar, tobacco, timber, hides and skins. The Central railway handles manganese ore, cotton and timber. The Eastern railway helps to transport rice, jute, coal, mica, manganese ore, iron ore, and fertilizer. The Western railway has newly started the construction of the Konkan railway 760 km. long. This zone handles the transport of cotton, oilseed, salt and mica.

Density of railways : The Great Plains of Uttar Pradesh, Bihar and West Bengal have adequate density of rail lines. The absence of hills and the level nature of the plains help in the laying of track. But the danger of floods and the cost of bridges are a drawback. The density is maximum in the coal fields of Jharia and Raniganj. Railways have made a headway in the mountain topography of Darjeeling and Simla. There are metro trains running between Esplanade and Bhavanipur in Calcutta covering a distance of 3.5, km connecting 5 stations. Another stretch of 2.2 km runs between Dum Dum and Belgachia.

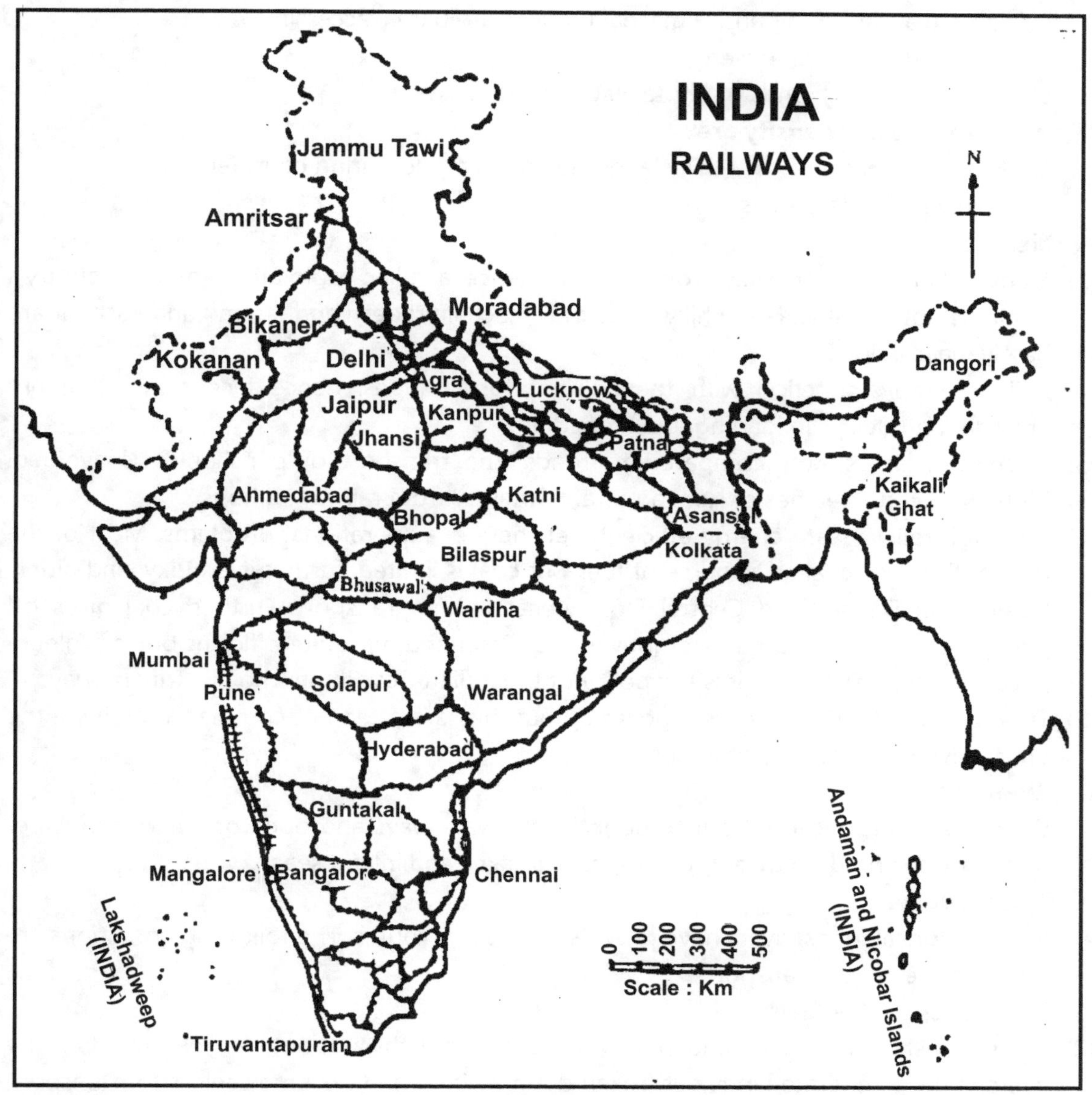

Map. 4.3

- In contrast is the Peninsular region where the density is reduced due to the broken topography and steeper gradients. Tunnels have to be built and in some places a 'banking' engine is necessary to pull the load on a steeper up-climb. Relief clearly dictates the laying of tracks in South India.

The areas with very few railways are :

1. North Eastern region,
2. Sikkim,

3.	Jammu and Kashmir and Himachal Pradesh are barely accessible
4.	Thar and Rajasthan deserts,
5.	The broken hilly lands of Chota Nagpur and Orissa.

The causes for lower density are :
1.	Broken topography with hilly landscape needing detouring considerably.
2.	Thinly populated areas.

Problems :
(1)	Many villages are far away from railways hence a fuller exploitation of the country's wealth is not possible. Many hilly areas of Himachal Pradesh and Jammu and kashmir are barely inaccessible.
(2)	Indian railways function with the help of four gauges, hence face trans shipment problem and delays in loading and unloading.
(3)	Since they are slower compared to roads, the transport of perishables is avoided. Moreover, vast stretches of rural areas are far away from railway stations.
(4)	Although railways are energy efficient, yet there are operational problems. Most of the locomotives use coal as a source of fuel. But coal is limited, further it is bulky, and highly localised in Eastern and Central India, necessitating transport. Further, coal gives off plenty of pollutants. Some locomotives use diesel and are quite efficient but petroleum prices are high. Therefore it is the policy of the Indian Government to electrify railways.
(5)	The wage bills of the railways is going up but they are often not commensurate with the productivity or efficiency of its services.

(III) Waterways :
•	Water transport is carried out through inland waterways and open ocean. Inland water transport is carried on through rivers, canals, lakes and inland seas.

River Transport :
•	Since historical times, rivers have provided transport routes. The following conditions are ideal for river water transport :
(1)	The river should be deep.
(2)	The rivers should carry an adequate volume of water throughout the year. Many of the rivers in the temperate lands get frozen during winter and become useless for transport, e.g. the St. Lawrence river in North America is frozen for about 5 months in a year and thus cannot be used for transport. The rivers that get water from seasonal rainfall swell during the rainy season and may prove dangerous for navigation. They carry very little water in the dry period and cannot be used for transport. The rivers of Peninsular India, like Godavari and Krishna, are of this type.
(3)	The rivers should not have rapids or waterfalls.
(4)	The rivers should not have many meanders. Meanders make circuitous and lengthy.
(5)	The rivers should be free from large deposits of alluvium. Due to large deposition of alluvium or silting, the rivers become shallow and become useless for large ships.

(6) The rivers should flow through areas of hospitable climate having high densities of population.

(7) The rivers should be long so that they can be used for long journeys.

Canal Transport :

* In some parts of the world, canals are used as waterways. They are either fed by reservoirs that are built in the mountainous areas or by rivers. Many canals are built to connect two major rivers and thus provide a network of cheap waterways. Canals are not subject to floods, they carry the same volume of water throughout the year and are not affected by deposition of sediments.

Major Inland Waterways :

Europe : The major rivers of Europe flow from south to north. These rivers are deep, carry water throughout the year and the seasonal fluctuation in their volume is low. Their mouths are open to traffic as alluvium is not deposited as is the case with deltas. Several rivers in Europe are linked to one another by canals and these rivers and canals have formed a dense network of inland water transport in Europe. The rivers in Europe flow through highly industriallsed, commercially important and densely populated areas. Industries require a constant supply of bulky, cheap raw material and have to dispatch manufactured goods to the markets. Rivers provide cheap waterways to transport raw material and manufactured goods. These rivers are the rivers Rhine, Loire, Seine, Meuse, Rhone, Ems, Weser, Elbe and Oder.

The Rhine river :

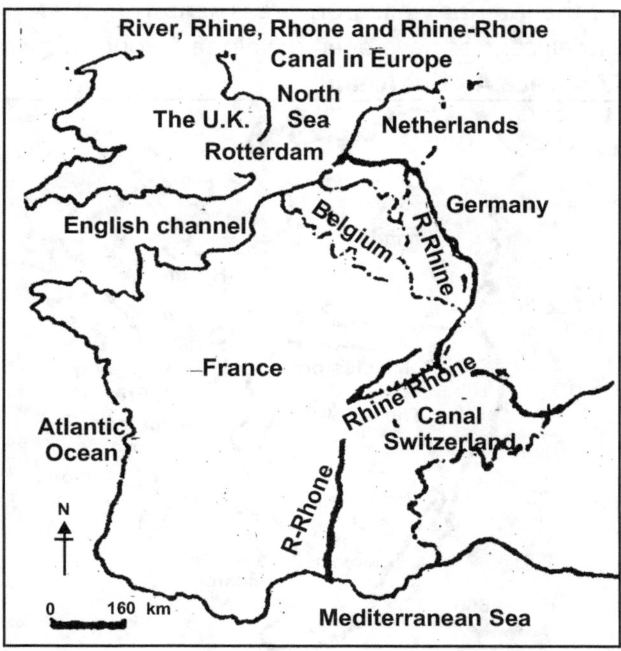

Map. 4.4

- This is the major waterway in Europe The Rhine is the most intensively used navigable river in the world. It is navigable from the port on the North Sea to Basle in Switzerland for a distance of 800 km. It is linked to the river Rhone and to the Mediterranean Sea by Rhine Rhone Canal. The Rhine is free from floods, ice and fluctuations in volume of water. The river flows through the highly, industrialized areas of West Europe. Petroleum, iron-ore, cotton, wool, food-grains, coal., timber, wood-pulp and several such commodities are carried from its mouth to the regions where they are needed while chemicals, fertilisers, steel products, machinery and manufactured goods are carried from these industrialised areas to the mouth and so to the world markets.

- Several canals built in Europe link the rivers e.g. Mitteland canal joins the rivers, Ems, Weser and Elbe. The Keil Canal, the Ludwig Canal, the Albert Canal and several others serve this same purpose and provide a dense network of cheap waterways.

North America

The Great-St. Lawrence Waterway :

The Great Lakes - St. Lawrence sea-way consisting of the St. Lawrence river, canals and Five Great Lakes of Superior, Michigan, Huron, Ontario and Erie forms the most important inland water-way in the world. It is 3760 km long and connects the Atlantic coastal areas with the interior of North America and large ocean-going vessels are able to reach to towns situated on the western shores of Lake Superior. There are several falls and rapids between the lakes. These have been avoided by the construction of canals and locks. This is the busiest inland waterway in the world and is used to carry wheat, wood, fur, milk products to the eastern coastal areas. Coal is transported from the eastern regions of the U.S.A. to the industrialised centres of the interior while iron-ore is sent from these regions to the eastern areas. 'Numerous industrial, centres have been developed along this waterways.

Inland Waterways of America Arctic Ocean

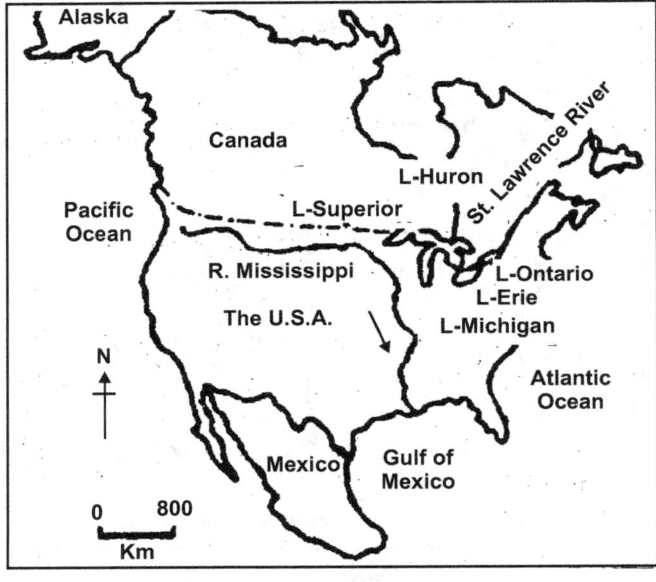

Map 4.5

The Mississippi river

- The river Mississippi flows north to south in the U.S.A. and joins the Gulf of Mexico. The tributaries of the rivers like the Ohio Illinois. and the Red together with the major river Missourie form the second most important waterway in the U. S. A. This water system has linked the wheat producing region near the Great Lakes and the coal producing regions of the Appalachians. Coal, petroleum and manufactured goods move through this waterway.

South America : The Amazon is one of the mightiest rivers of the world and is utilized by Brazil, Bolivia, Peru and Columbia for transport. Unfortunately it is not utilized on a large scale because its basin is covered by dense forests and is thus sparsely populated.

- The Plata-Parana-Paraguay waterway is the busiest waterway in South America. The other navigable rivers are the Magadalena in Colombia and the Orinoco in Venezuela. These rivers are utilised to carry rubber, Brazilian nuts, balata, iron-ore and manganese to the ports.

Russian Federation : The major inland waterways of the country lie in the European zone. The rivers that flow in the Asiatic part like the Ob, Yenisei and Lena flow towards the Arctic Ocean which is ice-bound for about 10 months of the year and these rivers also remain frozen for the greater part of the year.

- In its European part, the Volga is the most important waterway. The importance of the Volga river has been greatly increased due to its widening and deepening. The other important rivers are the Dnieper, Donetz, Don and Kama. Due to the construction of various canals like the Volga-Don Canal, Moscow has become an inland "port of five seas".

Asia : Inland waterways provide the chief means of transportation in Asia where roads and railways are not well developed. The major inland waterways are found in China, Myanmar and India.

- The Yangtze Kiang is by far the most important navigable river in China that links the interior regions of China with the Pacific Ocean. Ocean-going vessels can travel up to Nanking. This river flows through the highly developed and prosperous agricultural region of China. Food-stuffs, minerals, forest products and manufactured goods move along the river. River Si Kiang, Hwang Ho and the Sungari are also used on a smaller scale for navigation.

- In Myanmar the river Irrawaddy is navigable by large ships up to Bhamo and is used to carry oil,' food-grains and wood.

India : India has numerous long rivers but the country has small inland waterways because of the following reasons :

(1) The rivers of peninsular India are rain fed and hence have large fluctuations in the volume of water. Many rivers like Godavari are navigable only in their lower courses.

(2) The Himalayan rivers like the Gangs have become shallow due to continuous silting and are now unable to accommodate large ships.

(3) The Northern Great Plain has a dense net-work of roads and railways. The rivers have now lost their former importance due to more modern and efficient means of land transport.

(4) Most of the large rivers in India join the ocean through deltas which suffer from heavy silting.

- The major inland waterways in India are formed by the Ganga, the Brahmaputra and their tributaries; Mahanadi, Godavari and their canals; the Kayals or Lagoons in Kerala; Zuari and Mandovi rivers in Goa and the Buckingham Canal in Tamil Nadu and, Andhra Pradesh.

Ocean Transport :

- Though oceans provide vast waterbodies for transport, ships usually follow certain well defined tracks, known as ocean routes. Ocean routes play an important role in international trade and commerce. In recent times, large ocean liners which are able to carry huge quantities of goods at a time have been introduced in ocean transport. They save fuel and provide cheap means of transport. The major commodities that are carried through these routes are minerals, mineral oil, timber, agricultural products, wool, hides, heavy agricultural, industrial and transport machinery, cotton textiles and manufactured goods. Water transport is not very important for carrying passengers as journeys by ocean are slow and tedious.

The following are the peculiarities of ocean routes :

(1) As far as possible, the ocean routes follow the Great Circle Route which provides the minimum distance between any two places on the surface of the earth.

(2) The routes avoid areas having foggy or stormy weather. Ships usually follow the wind systems in order to save time and fuel.

(3) Waterways also avoid those parts of the oceans which are frequented by icebergs in spring and early summer, as these can be dangerous.

(4) Ocean-routes always touch ports-of-call where ships are able to take fresh supplies of fuel, water and food.

(5) Ocean-routes are chosen in such a way that they join ports that can carry out export and import of goods.

(6) Where ocean routes are laid through canals like the Suez or the Panama, the trading companies have to pay heavy taxes to the countries where these canals lie. Hence only costly or perishable commodities are sent through such short-cut ways while the bulky commodities are carried along the longer routes in order to minimise overall costs.

The major Ocean Routes in the World

The following are the major ocean routes of the world-

(1) The North Atlantic Route : This route is the busiest ocean route in the world. It joins the western coastal areas of Europe with the eastern coastal areas of North America. Both Western Europe and Eastern U.S.A. are densely populated, highly commercialised and industrialised regions. Hence this route carries goods on large scale. However, it has lost its previous importance of carrying passengers, as nowadays, people prefer to travel by air.

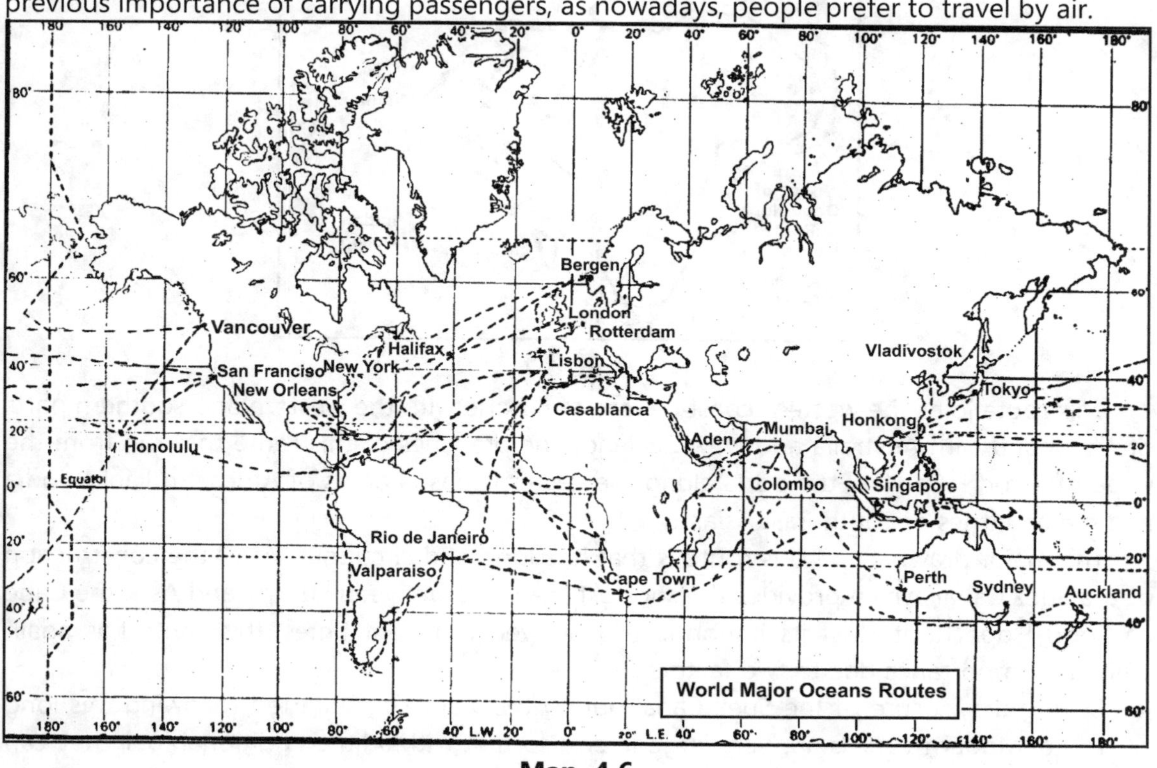

Map. 4.6

Rotterdam, Glasgow, Copenhagen, Manchester, London. Southampton and Oslo are major European ports which export various manufactured goods of high value, including machinery, as well as products like wine, jewellery and other luxury goods.

Ports along the North American coast includes Quebec, Montreal, Halifax, St. John. Boston. New York, Baltimore and New Orleans, A large variety of products is sent to the European market through these ports. They include wheat, wheat flour, tobacco, maize, cotton, timber, pulp, paper, dairy products, fish, machinery, vehicles, chemicals and other manufactured goods.

This waterway has numerous natural harbours where the water is deep enough to accommodate large ships. One drawback of this route is that the weather near New Foundland is foggy due to the meeting of the warm Gulf stream and the cool Labrador

Current. Further during spring and early summer, ice-bergs float southward with the Labrador Current. Hence during this period. ships follow a more southerly route.

(2) The Cape of Good Hope Route

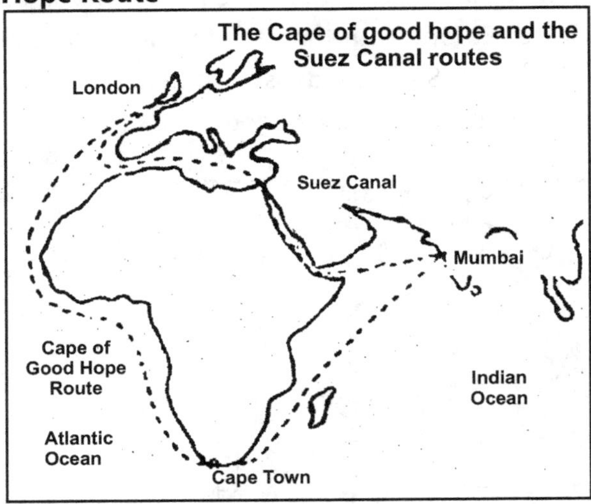

Map. 4.7

This route joins the western coastal areas of Europe with the western and southern parts of Africa and with Australia and New Zealand. The branches of this route that run from the Cape of Good Hope link the ports along the eastern coastal areas of Africa, Sri Lanka, India and the countries of South-East Asia.

The major drawback of this route is that it is long and circuitous. After the construction of the Suez Canal, which provides the shortest sea route between Europe and Asia, the Cape of Good Hope Route lost its importance. However, in recent times, this route has again gained its importance due to two factors :

(a) During the closure of the Suez Canal during the wars, ships started following this long route. Modern vessels are very large in size so that with a little additional fuel, they can carry a, much larger volume of freight at a cheaper rate. The Suez Canal is unable to accommodate Wiese large ships. Moreover, ships have to pay a heavy duty to the Egyptian Government for the use of the canal. hence, the ships use the Cape of Good Hope Route.

(b) Many of the South African countries have started producing minerals on a large scale and these have a constant and ever-increasing demand in the European market. Thus this route is brought into greater use.

The major ports along this route are London, Liverpool, Lisbon, Port Elizabeth, Cape Town, Colombo, Adelaide, Melbourne, Sydney and Brisbane.

African ports export a variety of minerals like gold, copper, diamonds, tin, chromium. manganese and palm-oil, hardwood, hides, skin and wool to Europe; Australian ports send wheat, wool and dairy products to Europe. European countries send manufactured goods to the African countries and to Australia.

(3) The Mediterranean-Suez-Asiatic Route

This route links the European countries with Australia and the Asian countries. This route, which passes through the Suez Canal, is the shortest route between these two regions. The canal has for instance, reduced the distance between Mumbai and London by 7200 km. It has thus provided short-route and minimised the time required and the transportation cost of the journey.

The Suez Canal : The Suez Canal was constructed across the narrow Isthmus of Suez. It was designed by the French Engineer, Ferdinand de Lessees. The construction took 10 years and was completed in 1869. This canal links the Mediterranean Sea with the Red Sea. It is 160 km. long, 66 m. broad and 11 m. deep. The canal lies at sea level. The Egyptian government nationalised this canal is 1956 and accordingly, ships passing through the canal have to pay a toll to A Egyptian government. Everyday, nearly 45 ships cross the canal, taking about 10 to 12 hours to do so.

The ports on the Suez Route are London, Liverpool, Lisban, Marseilles, Naples, Port Said, Aden, Mumbai, Colombo, Singapore, Perth, Adelaide, Melbourne and Sydney.

The significance of this route lies in the fact that it links the highly industrialised regions of Western Europe with the agricultural lands of Asia and Australia. Both Asia and Australia are rich in agricultural commodities and mineral resources, Western Europe is in need of raw materials for its industries and at the same time of markets for its manufactured goods.

Australia and the Asian countries export wool, hides, milk products, rubber, tea, coffee, oil-seeds, jute, spices, sugar, silk, foodgrains and cotton textile to the European countries and import locomotives, machinery, chemicals and other manufactured goods from them. Today the Suez Canal Route has lost its previous importance due to the following factors :

(i)   Political instability in the Suez Canal region.

(ii) Large size of the ships which are unable to pass through the canal.

(iii) Heavy toll levied by the Egyption Government.

(4) The Panama Canal Route

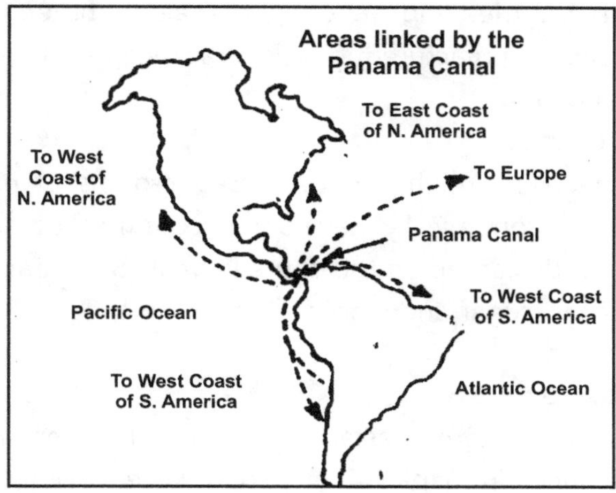

Fig. 4.8

Before the construction of the Panama Canal, ships travelling from the eastern coasts of the U. S. A. to the western coast had to circumnavigate the entire continent of South America. The canal opened a new door between the Atlantic and the pacific Ocean and is virtually "the gateway to the Pacific".

The Panama Canal : The Panama Canal is constructed through the narrow Isthmus of Panama. It was opened to traffic in 1914. This canal is 75 km long, 13 m. deep and the width varies between 100 and 330 metres. The maximum height of the canal is 28 m. above sea level, hence locks are provided to maintain the water level in the canal. Everyday nearly 48 ships pass through the canal taking about 6 to 8 hours to cross it. This canal is owned by the Panama government.

The Panama Canal has provided a short route connecting the following areas :

(a) The eastern and the western coastal areas of the U. S A.

(b) The eastern coastal areas and the western coastal areas of Canada.

(c) The western countries of South America like Chile, Peru, Bolivia and the eastern coasts of the U. S. A. and Canada.

(d) The eastern countries of South America like Brazil and Argentina and western coastal areas of the U. S. A. and Canada.

(e) The western coastal areas of South America and the western coastal areas of West European countries.

The Panama Canal route has proved beneficial to the home trade of the U. S. A. The western coastal areas of the U. S. A. send wheat, softwood, pulp, timber to the eastern states while the eastern U. S. A. sends back chemicals, fertilizers, a variety of manufactured goods and machinery.

The Panama route is responsible for the opening up of mines in the western countries of South America. These countries export copper, iron-ore, lead, nitrates to eastern U.S.A. and the West European countries and import chemicals, fertilizers, transportation equipment. mining machinery and manufactured. goods. Brazil exports hardwood, coffee and tropical fruits to the Western U. S. A.

(5) South Atlantic Route :

This route connects the highly industrialised regions of eastern North America and Western Europe with economically developing countries of eastern South America and Western Africa. The trade carried on this route is small. Brazil and Argentina send hardwood, rubber, coffee, bananas, sugar and wool to Europe and the U. S. A. imports coal machinery and manufactured goods.

(6) Trans-Pacific Route :

This route links the western coastal ports of North America with the countries of East and South-East Asia. including Japan, China, South Korea, Hongkong. Malaysia and Australia. The trade carried through this route is small because of the following reasons :

(i) There are very few islands in the Pacific Ocean where ships can refuel and take on food and water supplies.

(ii) The western region of North America is not a highly industrialised region.

North America sends wheat, wood, wood-pulp, newsprint, milk products and machinery to the Asian countries through the ports of Vancouver, Seatle, San Francisco, and Los Angeles-, South-East Asian countries mainly export agricultural commodities, e. g. rubber, tea, coffee, palm-oil, teak and copra. China exports silk while Japan exports silk. textiles and manufactured goods.

AIR TRANSPORT

Airways are developed mainly in the highly industrialised regions of the world like the U.S.A. and the Western Europe.

North America : The U. S. A. and Canada are both large and prosperous countries where airways play an important role in transporting passengers, perishable products like fruits, flowers, meat, mail and costly machinery. Both freight and passenger traffic is important because the airways have linked the distant parts of these countries. In all there are 9000 aerodromes in the U.S.A. Los Angeles, San Francisco, Boston, New York, Washigton D. C. are its busiest airports. Trans-World Air Lines and Pan American Airlines are the major air corporations in the U.S.A. Trans-Canadian Airline is the busiest air company in Canada., The major airports in Canada are the Montreal, Toronto and Vancouver.

Europe : The highly industrialised, commercially important and densely populated countries of West Europe have several important international, airports like Rome. Madrid, Paris, Vienna, London and Berlin. Air transport is important in Europe and passengers, mail and freight are regularly carried by the airways. Airways link the different parts of the world. Several European countries have their own airlines. The most important are British Airways, Lufthansa and S.A.S (run by Scandinavian countries).

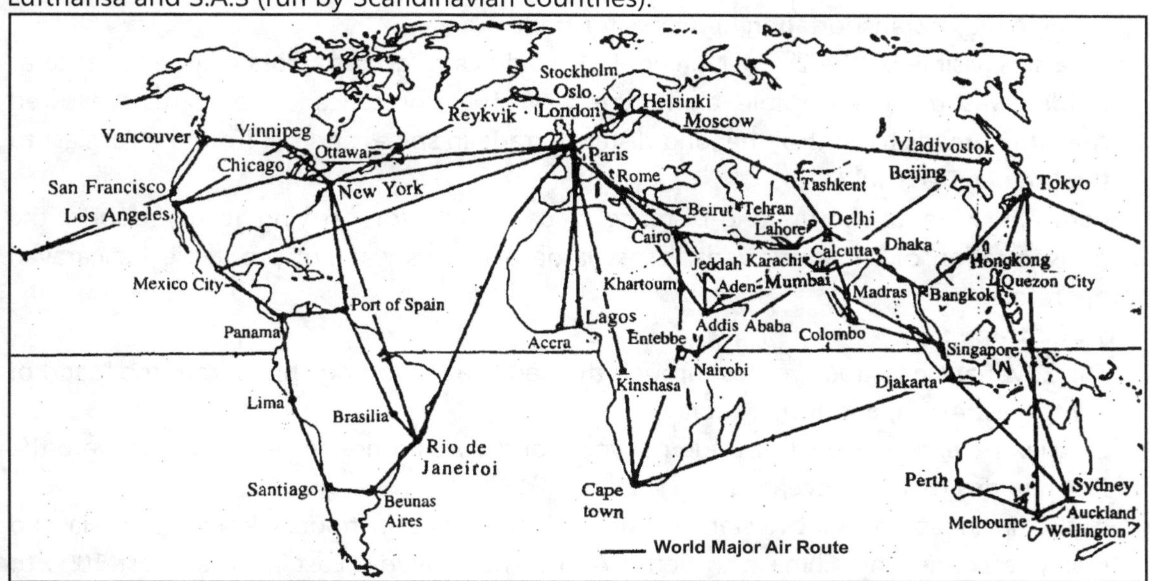

Map. 4.9

Russian Federation : Moscow is the hub of the airways which links the major industrial and administrative centres of the country. Though the airways are well-developed in European parts of the Russian Federaden, they are equally important in Asiatic part, where due to large size of landmass and very cold and long winters and resultant covered areas, airways are used to transport passengers, mail, medicines, etc.

India : Since, Independence, India has made rapid progress in air transport. Air India operates long distance international flights while Indian Airlines operates flights within the country. Mumbai (Chhatrapati Shivaji), Calcutta (Dum Dum). Delhi (Indira Gandhi), Chennai (Meenambakkam) and Tiruvananthapuram are major international airports. Due to low standard of living of people, the air transport is not much developed in India.

4.3.2 Types of Trade Routes - Silk Route, CPCC etc.

Trade route (Meaning)

- A trade route is a logistical network identified as a series of pathways and stoppages used for the commercial transport of cargo.
- Allowing goods to reach distant markets, a single trade route contains long distance arteries, which may further be connected to smaller networks of commercial and noncommercial transportation routes. Among notable trade routes was the Amber Road.
- During modern times, commercial activity shifted from the major trade routes of the Old World to newer routes between modern nation-states.

Development of early routes :

- The period from the middle of the 2nd millennium BCE to the beginning of the Common Era Southeast Asia, Western Asia, the Mediterranean, China, and the Indian subcontinent develop major transportation networks for trade.
- Caravans, visible by the 2nd millennium BCE, could carry goods across a large distance as fodder was mostly available along the way. The domestication of camels allowed Arabian nomads to control the long distance trade in spices and silk from the Far East to the Arabian Peninsula.
- Caravans were useful in long-distance trade largely for carrying luxury goods, the transportation of cheaper goods across large distances was not profitable for caravan operators.

Maritime trade :

- The Egyptians had trade routes through the Red Sea, importing spices from the "Land of Punt" (East Africa) and from Arabia.
- In Asia, the earliest Neolithic trade networks of the Austronesian peoples, who were the first humans to invent ocean-going ships.
- It also included the long distance routes of Austronesian traders from Indonesia and Malaysia connecting China with South Asia and the Middle East since at least 1000 to 600 BC.

- It helped in sprending Southeast Asian spices and Chinese goods to the west, as well as the spread of Hinduism and Buddhism to the east.
- This route would later become known as the Maritime Silk Road.
- South Asia had many maritime trade routes which connected it to Southeast Asia, thereby making the control of one route resulting in maritime monopoly difficult.
- Bulk Commodity Trade became possible for the Romans in the 2nd century BCE. A Roman trading vessel could span the Mediterranean in a month at one-sixtieth the cost of over-land routes.

Historic trade routes :

(I) Combined land and waterway routes

(a) Pre-Columbian trade :

- The flow of goods across the Andean slopes was controlled by institutions distributing locations to local groups, who were then free to access them for trading.
- A maritime exchange system stretched from the west coast of Mexico to southernmost Peru, trading mostly in Spondylus, which represented rain and fertility and was considered the principal food of the gods by the people of the Inca empire.

(II) Predominantly overland routes :

(a) Silk Road :

- "Along the Silk Roads, technology traveled, ideas were exchanged, and friendship and understanding between East and West were experienced for the first time on a large scale.
- Among the frequented routes of the Silk Route was the Burmese route which extended from Bhamo, which served as a path for Marco Polo's visit to Yunnan and Indian Buddhist missions to Canton in order to establish Buddhist monasteries.

(b) Grand Trunk Road :

- The Grand Trunk Road – connecting Chittagong in Bangladesh to Peshawar in Pakistan – has existed for over two and a half millennia.
- This road has been a strategic artery with fortresses, halting places, wells, post offices, milestones and other facilities. Part of this route coincided with the Silk Road in Pakistan.
- This highway is associated with emperors Chandragupta Maurya and Sher Shah Suri.
- Bridges, pathways and newer inns were constructed by the British for the first thirty-seven years of their reign since the occupation of Punjab in 1849.

(c) Amber Road :

- The Amber Road was a European trade route associated with the trade and transport of Amber. Amber was in high demand for ornamental purposes around the Mediterranean.
- Towns along the Amber Road began to rise steadily during the 1st century CE.

- Under the reign of Tiberius Caesar Augustus, the Amber Road was straightened and paved according to the prevailing urban standards and Roman towns began to appear along the road.

(d) Via Maris :

- Via Maris ("the way of the sea,") was an ancient highway used by the Romans and the Crusaders.
- Due to the biblical significance of this ancient route, many attempts to find its present-day location have been made by Christian pilgrims.

(e) Trans Saharan trade :

- People of West Africa operated a sophisticated network of trade, usually under the authority of a monarch.
- Sophisticated mechanisms for the economic and political development of the involved African areas were in place before Islam further strengthened trade, towns and government in western Africa.
- The powerful Saharan tribes, later adapting to Islam and Arab cultures, controlled the channels to western Africa by making efficient use of horse-drawn vehicles and pack animals.

(III) Predominantly maritime routes :

(a) Austronesian maritime trade network

- The first significant maritime trade network in the Indian Ocean was by the Austronesian peoples of Island Southeast Asia, who built the first ocean-going ships.
- They established trade routes with Southern India and Sri Lanka as early as 1500 BC, ushering an exchange of material culture (like catamarans, outrigger boats, sewn-plank boats, and paan) and cultigens (like coconuts, sandalwood, bananas, and sugarcane); as well as connecting the material cultures of India and China.
- This trade network to reached as far as Africa and the Arabian Peninsula, resulting in the Austronesian colonization of Madagascar by the first half of the first millennium AD.
- It continued later becoming the Maritime Silk Road. This trade network also included smaller trade routes within Island Southeast Asia, including the lingling-o jade network, and the trepanging network.

(b) Roman-India routes :

- The Ptolemaic dynasty had started Greco-Roman maritime trade contact with India using the Red Sea ports.
- The Indians were present in Alexandria and the Christian and Jewish settlers from Rome continued to live in India long after the fall of the Roman empire, which resulted in Rome's loss of the Red Sea ports.

(c) Hanseatic trade :

- German traders became prominent in the Baltic and the North Sea regions.

- Philippe Dollinger associates the downfall of the Hansa to an alliance between Lübeck, Hamburg and Bremen, which outshadowed the older institution. He further sets the date of dissolution of the Hansa at 1630 and concludes that the Hansa was almost completely forgotten by the end of the 18th century.

(d) From the Varangians to the Greek :

- The trade route from the Varangians to the Greeks was a trade route that connected Scandinavia, Kievan Rus' and the Byzantine Empire.
- This route allowed traders along the route to establish a prosperous trade with Byzantium, and prompted some of them settled in the territories of present-day Belarus, Russia and Ukraine.
- Then it followed the Volkhov River, past the towns of Staraya Ladoga and Velikiy Novgorod, crossed Lake Ilmen, and up the Lovat River.
- From there, ships had to be portaged to the Dnieper River near Gnezdovo. A second route from the Baltic to the Dnieper was along the Western Dvina (Daugava) between the Lovat and the Dnieper in the Smolensk region, and along the Kasplya River to Gnezdovo.

(e) Maritime republics' Mediterranean trade :

- The growing independence of some coastal cities gave them a leading role in this commerce: Maritime Republics of Venice, Genoa, Amalfi, Pisa and Republic of Ragusa developed their own "empires" in the Mediterranean shores. Till the 15th century, they held the monopoly of European trade with the Middle East. The silk and spice trade, involving spices, incense, herbs, drugs and opium, made these Mediterranean city-states phenomenally rich.
- Spices were imported from Asia and Africa. Muslim traders – mainly descendants of Arab sailors dominated maritime routes throughout the Indian Ocean.

(f) Spice Route :

- As trade between India and the Greco-Roman world increased spices became the main import from India to the Western world, bypassing silk and other commodities.
- The Indian commercial connection with South East Asia proved important to the merchants of Arabia and Persia during the 7th and 8th centuries.
- On the orders of Manuel I of Portugal, four vessels under the command of navigator Vasco da Gama rounded the Cape of Good Hope reached Calicut. The wealth of the Indies was now open for the Europeans and the Portuguese Empire was one of the early European empires to grow from spice trade.

(g) Maritime Silk Road :

- The Maritime Silk Road refer to the maritime section of historic Silk Road that connects China, Southeast Asia, the Indian subcontinent, Arabian peninsula, Somalia and all the way to Egypt and finally Europe.

- The Maritime Silk Road developed from the earlier Austronesian spice trade networks of Islander Southeast Asians with Sri Lanka and Southern India (established 1000 to 600 BCE), as well as the jade industry trade in lingling-o artifacts from the Philippines in the South China Sea (c. 500 BCE).

(h) Modern routes :

- Map of the Arctic region showing the Northeast Passage, the Northern Sea Route within it, and the Northwest Passage.

- Newer means of transport led to the establishment of new routes, and countries opened up borders to allow trade in mutually agreed goods as per the prevailing free trade agreement.

Modern maritime routes :

- There has been a consistent shift from land based trade to sea-based trade.

- Modern maritime trade routes. i.e. opening of the Suez Canal altered British interactions with the colonies of the British Empire.

- Other waterways, like the Panama Canal played an important role in the histories of many nations.

- Inland water transportation remained significantly important even as the advent of railroads and automobiles resulted in a steady decline of canals.

- Waterway commerce was historically important to Europe, particularly to Russia.

- The Silk Road was a network of trade routes which connected the East and West, and was central to the economic, cultural, political, and religious interactions between these regions from the 2nd century BCE to the 18th century.

- This refers to the land routes connecting East Asia and Southeast Asia with South Asia, Persia, the Arabian Peninsula, East Africa and Southern Europe.

- The Silk Road derives its name from the lucrative trade in silk carried out along its length, beginning in the Han dynasty in China (207 BCE–220 CE).

- The Silk Road trade played a significant role in the development of the civilizations of China, Korea, Japan, the Indian subcontinent, Iran, Europe, the Horn of Africa and Arabia, opening long-distance political and economic relations between the civilizations.

- Though silk was the major trade item exported from China, many other goods and ideas were exchanged.

- The Silk Road was initiated and globalized by Chinese exploration and conquests in Central Asia.

- A maritime Silk Route opened up between Chinese-controlled Giao Chi (centred in modern Vietnam, near Hanoi), probably by the 1st century. It extended, via ports on the coasts of India and Sri Lanka, all the way to Roman-controlled ports in Roman Egypt and the Nabataean territories on the northeastern coast of the Red Sea.

- Maës Titianus penetrated farthest east along the Silk Road from the Mediterranean world, probably with the aim of regularising contacts and reducing the role of middlemen, during one of the lulls in Rome's intermittent wars with Parthia, which repeatedly obstructed movement along the Silk Road.

- Although the Silk Road was initially formulated during the reign of Emperor Wu of Han (141–87 BCE), it was reopened by the Tang Empire in 639 when Hou Junji conquered the Western Regions, and remained open for almost four decades.

- After conquests, the Tang dynasty fully controlled the Xiyu, which was the strategic location astride the Silk Road. This led the Tang dynasty to reopen the Silk Road.

- The Tang dynasty established a second Pax Sinica, and the Silk Road reached its golden age, whereby Persian and Sogdian merchants benefited from the commerce between East and West.

- The Silk Road represents an early phenomenon of political and cultural integration due to inter-regional trade.

- The Sogdians dominated the East-West trade after the 4th century up to the 8th century, with Suyab and Talas ranking among their main centres in the north.

- The Silk Road gave rise to military states of nomadic origins in North China, ushered the Nestorian, Manichaean, Buddhist, and later Islamic religions into Central Asia and China.

- The Round city of Baghdad between 767 and 912 was the most important urban node along the Silk Road.

- At the end of its glory, the routes brought about the largest continental empire ever, the Mongol Empire, with its political centres strung along the Silk Road.

- The Mongol expansion throughout the Asian continent from around 1207 to 1360 helped bring political stability and re-established the Silk Road (via Karakorum and Khanbaliq).

- The fragmentation of the Mongol Empire loosened the political, cultural, and economic unity of the Silk Road. Turkmeni marching lords seized land around the western part of the Silk Road from the decaying Byzantine Empire. After the fall of the Mongol Empire, the great political powers along the Silk Road became economically and culturally separated.

- The silk trade continued to flourish until it was disrupted by the collapse of the Safavid Empire in the 1720s.

- After an earthquake that hit Tashkent in Central Asia in 1966, the city had to rebuild itself. Although it took a huge toll on their markets, this commenced a revival of modern silk road cities.

- The Eurasian Land Bridge, a railway through China, Kazakhstan, Mongolia and Russia, is sometimes referred to as the "New Silk Road".

Routes :

- The Silk Road consisted of several routes. As it extended westwards from the ancient commercial centres of China, the overland, intercontinental Silk Road divided into northern and southern routes bypassing the Taklamakan Desert and Lop Nur.

Maritime route

- Maritime Silk Road or Maritime Silk Route refer to the maritime section of historic Silk Road that connects China to Southeast Asia, Indonesian archipelago, Indian subcontinent, Arabian peninsula, all the way to Egypt and finally Europe.

4.4 NEW TRENDS IN THE MEANS AND MODES OF TRANSPORTATION

- Transportation is crucial because it paves the way for growth and exchange. Because of international shipping lines and airfreight services, the world is now a global village because collaboration between various businesses around the world is made possible and a lot more feasible with transportation.

The Buzz About Transportation Digitalization

- Transportation business processes from administration, contracting, production, and other operations continue to digitally evolve.
- More than half of transportation companies expect that digitalization will improve their profitability.
- By redesigning services and modifying products, companies are able to produce better vehicles, air crafts, and ships.
- Tapping new talents that have been educated with the latest engineering concepts help in boosting the transportation industry.
- Digitalization has forever been present since the time Henry Ford crafted the first model T Ford car.
- Digitalization will always be a trend in the transportation industry year after year.

Persistent Shifts in International Trade :

- International trade is multi dimensional and rests on many outside factors. In the transportation industry, the persistent shifts in international trade have the capacity to influence local markets, such as what products will be imported, what will be sellable, and what needs more marketing work.
- Just as the US's influence is beginning to wane, China's economic expansion with the developing of trade routes show the country's influence. These massive shifts have impacted the transportation industry, with many manufacturers choosing to focus their attention on the developing countries.

Damaged Infrastructure

- Through out the world, countries have been suffering immensely from natural disasters.

- Hurricanes in the United States, massive earthquakes in Japan, or tsunamis ni Indonesia have impacted transportation infrastructure, which these countries are having difficulty recovering from.
- As a result, there has been a deeline in transportation production in these areas because they are more focused on recovery.

Environmental Considerations :

- Due to global warming and climate change that has impacted the globe, people have become more environmentally aware.
- People are now known to take the environment as a consideration in their transportation decisions.
- Electric cars that are seen as better for the environment because they emit less carbon emissions and consume lesser fossil fuels have increased in sales.
- People are making conscious efforts to lessen their carbon footprint by choosing to carpool or take public transport.
- Many people resort to walking, ride-sharing, taking their bikes, and the like to work, school, or other areas.

Telecommuting and Working from Anywhere :

- Computers and the Internet have made it possible for people from different parts of the globe to interact and engage in business.
- Being able to connect with digital resources and access work from anywhere is now a trend in the new generation.
- Majority of people who engage in this lifestyle have no need for transportation. In some areas, there has been a drop in sales because people who can telecommute to work no longer need them.
- On top of that, using the ride sharing option gives people a chance to socialize.

Software Driven Changes :

- The improvement of software has affected the transportation industry. Apps like Uber and Lyft make it possible for people to hire cars easily, so they not own one.
- On top of that, there are apps for private jets like JetSmarter, which is considered as the Uber for private flying. Apps have made it easy for people to book flights, bus tickets, and boat trips.
- Aside from that, automobile software built into the vehicles have also evolved. Now, there are many options built into the vehicle for the protection of the driver and occupants.

Safety Considerations

- Transportation has always been built with safety as a side from human error, things from within the machines itself can fall apart causing accidents.

- Boats, airplanes, buses, and trains, there are standards in place for these public transport services to be given permits.
- Manufacturers are always hard at work in delivering quality products and improving their technology.
- Even for private cars, maintenance and compliance with certain regulations are required.
- Modern cars have many features that keep the occupants safety i.e. standard seat belts and airbags, high speed alerts, temperature check, remote start for climate control, pedestrian and bike detection, hill start and hill descent assist, back up cameras, blind spot monitors, push start button, anti lock braking system, and many more.
- The safety of all human beings is the number one consideration in the transportation industry.

Next Generation GPS Services :
- GPS systems they have been present and functional for quite a few years now.
- Modern Gps Devices add functionality through its many updated features.
- The new GPS models offer so much more versatility, aside from the basic old functions, they can make adjustments for your trip by factoring in weather conditions, traffic reports, and road conditions on the chosen route.
- In terms of the aviation, locomotive, and shipping industries, the GPS system has allowed for each trip to be a lot more safer and precise in terms of calculating arrival dates.

Machine Driven Process Changes :
- Airplanes and boats have long been able to cruise on auto-pilot mode.
- There have been discussions about automated cars or driver-less vehicles. This has been a major project for the car industry. Self-driving automobiles are already here and are consistently being tested to make them market ready.
- Developers and manufacturers remain very optimistic about the progress, development, and growth of fully autonomous vehicles.
- There are many other trends in the transportation industry that have a great effect on consumers globally. After all, this industry is massive, with manufacturing plants in different countries around the world.
- Being aware of existing trends is helpful for the manufacturers and dealers, so they can make proper marketing strategies and forecasts.
- As for the consumers, it is also vital that they become aware of the existing trends and statistics.

Points to Remember

- Transport and communication is a major tertiary economic activity.
- Trade brings about exchange of goods between two regions.

- Types of commodities traded :
  - (i) Industrial raw materials
  - (ii) Food
  - (iii) Fuel
  - (iv) Manufacture and machinery
- The comparative volume of exports and imports determines the balance of trade.
- Some international organizations related to commerce : OPEC, EEC, (GATT) WTO, G-15 etc.
- Inter-regional trade refers to trade between regions within a country.
- International trade is trade between two nations on countries.
- Roads, Railways, Waterways and Airways are the major modes of transportation.
- Waterways provide the cheapest mode of transport.
- Ocean routes also have a large influence on the location are growth of Industries.
- The Trans-Siberian railway is the most important railway line in Russia.
- The major ocean routes in the world
  - (i) The North Atlantic Route
  - (ii) The cape of Good hope route
  - (iii) The Mediterranean sues - Asiatic Route
  - (iv) The sues canal route
  - (v) The Panama canal route
  - (vii) South Atlantic route
  - (viii) Trans-Pacific route
- Historic trade routes combined law and waterways :
  - (i) Incense route
  - (ii) Silk Road
  - (iii) Grand Trunk Road
  - (iv) Amber Road
  - (v) Via Maris
  - (vi) Trans Saharan trade
- Predominantly maritime routes :
  - (i) Anstronesial maritiare
  - (ii) Roman - India routed
  - (iii) Harseatic trade
  - (iv) From the varangians to the Greek
  - (v) Maritime Mediterranean trade
  - (vi) Spice route
  - (vii) Maritime silk road
  - (viii) Modern Route.

Questions for Discussion

Q. (I) Answer the following questions :

1. What is Trade ? What are the bases for development of Trade ?
2. What is the importance of Trade in Economic development ?
3. What are the types of Trade ? What are the advantages and disadvantages ?
4. What is the major direction of International trade ?
5. Name some International organizations related to commerce ?
6. What are the differences between Inter Regional Vs. International trade ?
7. What are the Advantages and Disadvantages of Transportation ?
8. What is the role of Transportation in commercial development ?
9. What are the Advantages and Disadvantages of Road transport ?
10. What are the Advantages and Disadvantages of Railways transport ?
11. What are the Advantages and Disadvantages of Air transport ?
12. What are the Advantages and Disadvantages of water transport ?
13. What are the major Inland waterways in the world ?
14. What are the types of Trade routes ?
15. What do you know about the silk trade route ?
16. What are the new trends in the means and modes of Transportation ?

Q. (II) Short Notes :

1. Trade
2. Types of Trade
3. Balance of Trade
4. OPEC
5. Interregional Trade
6. Transportation
7. Silk route
8. Roadways – Advantages
9. Railways – Disadvantages
10. Airways – Advantages
11. Waterways – Disadvantages